Life Lessons for Busy Moms

Also by Dorothy K. Breininger and Debby S. Bitticks
The Senior Organizer
Time Efficiency Makeover

Also by Lynn Benson
The Senior Organizer

Life Lessons for Busy Moms

7 Essential Ingredients to Organize and Balance Your World

Jack Canfield

Mark Victor Hansen

Dorothy K. Breininger, Debby S. Bitticks
and Lynn Benson

Health Communications, Inc.
Deerfield Beach, Florida

www.hcibooks.com
www.chickensoup.com

We would like to acknowledge the many publishers and individuals who granted us permission to reprint the cited material. (Note: The stories that were penned anonymously, that are in the public domain, or that were written by Jack Canfield, Mark Victor Hansen, Dorothy K. Breininger, Debby S. Bitticks, and Lynn Benson are not included in this listing.)

(Continued on page 333)

**Library of Congress Cataloging-in-Publication Data
is available from the Library of Congress.**

©2007 John T. Canfield and Hansen and Hansen LLC
ISBN-13: 978-0-7573-0557-3
ISBN-10: 0-7573-0557-1

Publisher: Health Communications, Inc.
3201 S.W. 15th Street
Deerfield Beach, FL 33442–8190

R-11-06

Cover design by Andrea Perrine Brower
Inside formatting by Dawn Von Strolley Grove

Too Busy

The dishes are still in the sink.
Dirty laundry is piled high.
Somehow the entire day,
Seemed to just fly by.
I made a "to-do" list.
I meant to follow through.
But there were other tasks,
That needed attention too.
Like cheering on my daughter,
As she took first steps into my arms,
Making sure she stayed safe,
From all potential harms.
Cuddling on the couch,
And reading a favorite story.
Helping her explore the world,
And marvel at all its glory.
So the chores will have to wait.
They aren't that important anyway.
Because I was simply too busy,
Loving my child today.

Sabrina A. Taylor

Contents

Essential Ingredient #3: Implement Creative Solutions (with an Organized Approach)

Essential Ingredient #4: Feed Your Soul

Essential Ingredient #7: Make Time to Slow Down

Acknowledgments

We wish to express our heartfelt gratitude to the following people who helped make this book possible.

From Debby: Special gratitude to my husband, Ken, who was constantly supportive with endless devotion to see this project through, and to my children, Shari, Michelle, Lynn, Sandi, Bryan, Tracey, and Kevin, and their spouses, C. J., Rick, Steven, J. T., Tamara, John, and Citlali who were all devoted and supportive in the development of this book. Thank you also to all of my precious grandchildren for the love and hugs you have given your own busy moms. And thank you to my sister Selma and my brother-in-law Bob.

From Lynn: Thank you to my husband, Steven, for the tremendous love, faith, and support you gave in seeing this book through, and to my daughters, Alana and Jenna, for your patience and inspiration, and for teaching me so much about how to live a full and enriched life as a busy mom.

From Dorothy: Thank you to my grandmother Lucia and Aunt Erna who taught my mom—who then taught me—how to make sense of my world by getting organized, prioritized, and then taking action. Thank you to Pat, Ed, Pam, Chris, Ron and my dear aunts, uncles, nieces, nephews, and friends for overlooking and later praising the daily plans, telephone appointments, and agendas—fraught with minute-to-minute activities and assignments during visits and trips.

Special acknowledgments to our core team:

Gillian Drake-White—Project Manager. Thank you for your complete dedication to the details of this project. While we were on the road, it was you who spent countless hours reviewing, repairing, reminding, and indeed leading us to stay focused.

Pat Brady—Editor. Thank you for your commitment to the written word despite unreasonable deadlines. Your attention to the editing of this book allowed all of us to express ourselves in a way that is palatable to our readers and acceptable to our publishers.

Lynn Benson—Head Writer and Coauthor. Thank you for drawing from your own experiences to generate the main content for this book. Without a doubt you are living the life of a busy mom, and we appreciate your leadership and drive to create a meaningful book that allows women all over the world to get organized and take care of their souls.

To our staff—We all thank you for your leadership each day in the areas for which you are responsible: David Factor and his family, Holly, Perry and Reina, for reorganizing your worlds so that we could make our projects successful; Angie Chiquette for organizing our financial world; Rick Cataldo (our webmaster genius) and his wife, Barbara, as well as everyone at DENOVO Medical Venture Marketing; John Shields for organizing our company to deliver more focused products and seminars; Chris Faltynek and her crew: Catalina Carter, Amber Kohler, Marisol Montoya, and Todd Silver for teaching our clients to organize their own time, space, and ideas; Pat Brady for organizing the words we speak and write and Jerry Krautman for the images we imagine; and Gillian Drake-White and Jeanette Brennan for their magical input, which positively impacts every aspect of our company. Also, a special thank-you to Michelle Brower, Cindy Moskovic, Anna Lissa Arvisu, and Bill White for their special contributions.

To our Chicken Soup mentors and publisher—Thank you to the busiest mom we know: Patty Aubery, president of Chicken Soup Enterprises, who led us to HCI and Peter Vegso, our risk-taking, insightful, and one-of-a-kind publisher and friend. Peter, we thank you for believing in us. And to our amazing coauthors and Chicken Soup creators, Jack Canfield and Mark Victor Hansen, who, in the face of their own tireless schedules, look every potential author in the eyes to tell them that they also have a book inside of them.

Thank you to Patty Hansen and Russ Kalmaski—the "go-to gurus" for assuring success for everyone involved in this project and every other project they touch and D'ette Corona and Barbara LoMonaco, our very seasoned and loyal guides through our first Chicken Soup experience. We also wish to thank Jack and Mark's staff who ensure the success of all of us: Veronica Romero, Teresa Esparza, Robin Yerian, Jesse Ianniello, Lauren Edelstein, Laurie Hartman, Patti Clement, Maegan Romanello, Noelle Champagne, Jody Emme, Debbie Lefever, Michelle Adams, Dee Dee Romanello, Shanna Vieyra, and Gina Romanello.

To those of you who are accountable to edit, market, coordinate, connect, collect, make, ship, represent or sell our books: Kim Weiss, Julie De La Cruz O'Hara, Pat Holdsworth, Michele Matriscini, Andrea Gold, Allison Janse, Carol Rosenberg, Katheline St. Fort, Cathy Slovensky, Terry Burke, Lori Golden, Kelly Maragni, Tom Galvin, Sean Geary, Patricia McConnell, Ariana Daner, Paola Fernandez-Rana, Larissa Hise Henoch, Lawna Patterson Oldfield, Andrea Perrine Brower, Anthony Clausi, Dawn Von Strolley Grove, Tom Sand, Claude Choquette, and Luc Jutras.

To our gracious and thoughtful panel of readers— Michelle Brower, Jennifer Brown, Jan Carey, Brenda LaMont, Colleen Lindsay, Kelly Mason, Nicola Mingins, Jo Pessin, Joyce Rapier, Pat Ritter, Kimberly Ryan, Jean Stewart, Jessica Stone, Stephanie Thompson, Erin Torson, and Christina Winting.

To our business affiliations—the organizations we belong to who support our ever-growing businesses. The opportunities you present to us allow us to learn more about our business. Thank you—National Association of Professional Organizers (NAPO), National Study Group on Chronic Disorganization (NSGCD), National Association of Women Business Owners (NAWBO), National Association of Female Executives (NAFE), Small Business Association (SBA), and Los Angeles Chamber of Commerce.

To our friends and colleagues who submitted their heartfelt stories, poems, quotes, and cartoons for possible inclusion in this book—while we were not able to use everything you sent in, we know that each submission reflected the amazing human being you are.

Sometimes the most important people can be overlooked when creating acknowledgments for a collaborative effort of this size. We are sorry if we missed your name and please know we do appreciate you very much.

Introduction

"I am a busy mom." This can be said in exasperation, echoing the weariness of late nights and early mornings spent caring for our families. It can be whispered in a hush, as our children settle in for an afternoon nap and we try to steal ten minutes for ourselves to read the newspaper. It can be yelled in celebration, proclaiming the exuberance and love we feel for our families. Anyway it's said, felt, or lived, the bottom-line truth is that if you picked up this book, you are, or probably know very well, a *busy mom*.

The magic of this book comes through when reading the mosaic of personal stories shared by *busy moms* about their triumphs, challenges, life-changing events, and even their practical ideas and solutions that can make a profound difference within very hectic days. When we embark on the amazing journey of motherhood with all its joys, chaos, and excitement, we have the opportunity to learn lessons and gain areas of expertise that can greatly benefit others if shared.

The stories throughout this book are combined with Essential Ingredients. Together they are intended to not only provide inspiration for us to achieve lifelong dreams and aspirations that we once thought were "impossible," but also to offer us very basic and practical organizing tips that can potentially transform our very hectic days—from the frenzied crazy moments to the enjoyable, zany, fun times we all yearn to share with our families.

Throughout our days, our own unique life experiences have shaped the way we think and have contributed to the manner in which we approach each new day as we strive to do our very best in all of the multiple roles that we play as moms, daughters, sisters, spouses, friends—and the list goes on!

In addition to the many helpful and practical tips throughout this book, it is our hope that readers will feel inspired to embrace and fulfill dreams that have not yet taken shape and set them into motion. We also deeply encourage *busy moms* to celebrate their accomplishments and the incredible job they all do each and every day. For those of us who are busy moms, we work so hard to be the best moms possible; it's time to recognize this in ourselves and celebrate our achievements as we continue on the path of the amazing experience of motherhood.

MAKE TIME TO NURTURE YOURSELF

Busy, busy, busy we pass the days
of our lives—gone all to soon.
Gone before we get to our dreams of creative
expressions, self-fulfillment, nurturing.

Carol Osborn

Reprinted by permission of Dan Rosandich ©2006.

LIFE LESSON #1

Celebrate Your Achievements as a Busy Mom

The more you praise and celebrate your life,
the more there is in life to celebrate.

Oprah Winfrey

How Did Mama Do It?

At least once a day I find myself standing somewhere in my house gazing skyward asking, "Mama, how did you do it?" Before she died, my mama raised twelve children. But if the truth be told, at least twice that many resided under her roof or under her wing at one time or another. Our house was always open to friends, extended family, neighbors, and more than once to total strangers.

Through it all Mama never lost her cool, never raised her voice, and never seemed to run out of steam. Before I had three children of my own, I figured I'd be just like her. Why wouldn't I? I have her genes and all those years of watching her in action. Let's face it—I had a tough act to follow.

I was the eleventh child. By the time I came along Mama had the house running like a well-oiled machine. I never stopped to wonder how she did it. I dropped my clothes in the hamper. They magically reappeared in my dresser. When I was hungry, there was food on the table. When I was dirty, a nice, hot bath appeared (often with three or four siblings, cousins, or neighborhood kids for company).

Mama made most of our clothes, served as PTA president,

room mother, president of the church counsel, looked in on elderly neighbors, threw the world's best birthday parties on little or no budget, left encouraging notes on my pillow when I needed them most, and when she wrapped Christmas presents, each one was unique. Yet, I remember her having all the time in the world to play with us, to talk to us and any one of our friends who was having a rough go of it.

She never seemed to be in a hurry, overwhelmed, or stressed, and no one ever heard her complain about all she had on her plate. I won't say the house was immaculate, but it was livable, and you just never knew who might be seated around our dinner table at night. Many a cousin or friend, when going through the rebellious teen years, moved in with us for a few months or a year while Mama secretly counseled their parents on the side. We were Catholic, and nuns and priests were often found in our living room late at night pouring their hearts out to my mom. After I went off to college, it wasn't unusual to call home and have one of my high school buddies answer the phone. When I asked them what they were doing at my house (didn't they realize I didn't live there anymore?), they'd answer, "Just hanging out with your mom."

One vivid memory I have of Mama involves my brother, Ken. The sixth child in our family, Ken was born with cerebral palsy, profound deafness, a gentle spirit, and a special spot in Mama's heart. On this day some ladies from the church were gathered in our living room enjoying polite conversation and cups of my mom's coffee. Mama noticed Ken was awake, excused herself to serve him breakfast, then rejoined the ladies. But when Ken went for a sip of grape juice, his arm experienced an involuntarily spasm, splattering dark purple juice all over two walls, the curtains and himself. He was mortified! Mama got up to take care of the mess and found him with his head hanging down, face beet red, apologizing over and over. She didn't miss a beat. Looking down in the cup, she saw that there were still a couple of inches of juice. She threw it on the only remaining clean wall, and told Ken, "You missed a spot."

That was my mama. I can just see Ken now, dissolving in laughter, forgetting all about his embarrassment as Mama got down on her knees to clean up the mess. Now, tell me those aren't big shoes to fill. I'm happy to report, though, that on good days I catch a glimpse of her in me. When my to-do list is a mile long and I realize one of my kids needs some attention, I manage to take a deep breath, invite him to "Come on—let's make some cookies." And begin a story that usually starts, "Did I ever tell you about the time my mama . . ." Just talking about her reminds me of how it felt to be on the receiving end of her patience and warmth, and I realize my children deserve nothing less.

I may never learn to sew. I'll probably always struggle with time management. And they'll have to find someone else to run the PTA this year, but when it comes to being a loving, devoted mom, I figure I'm ahead of the game, as long as I just follow Mama's blueprint.

Mimi Greenwood Knight

LIFE LESSON #1

Many of us busy moms get caught up in the "perfect mom syndrome." We try so hard and do so much to be the best mom possible. And even after all of our tireless efforts, many of us walk around feeling like we should be a "better mom." It's not until we have an opportunity to chat with other moms that we realize we are truly not alone with these thoughts and feelings. What can we do about this? For starters, the basic idea of celebrating our achievements as busy moms is a great place to begin! We tend to be too focused on what we're not doing right, on how to do things better; how incredible would it feel to start recognizing what we are doing right? Of course, we all know the importance of balance. We may do self-analysis on a regular basis on how we can better ourselves as moms and as human beings; after all, we all want to strive to be the best person possible. This is all very important, but again, the key is balance. It's great to evaluate what we could do better, but the trick is doing this without beating ourselves up. Then let's kick it up a notch and celebrate our achievements as busy moms. As women and moms, we often take pride in our strength to nurture and feel compassion toward others, but we tend to lack the ability to self-nurture and show compassion toward ourselves. We are so hard on ourselves!

Let's talk about those of us who are stay-at-home moms; let's think about what that's worth out in the marketplace. According to the 2004 U.S. Census Bureau Report, there are 5.5 million stay-at-home moms for the 41 million children under age 15 living with two parents.[1] Stay-at-home dads numbered only 147,000. Also consider that the 2004 median household income was $44,684. Findings based on a 90-hour workweek by Salary.com estimates that "fair wages for the typical stay-at-home mom would be over $90,000. This does not include overtime, which would account for another $25,000 to the wage."[2] Regina Robo, News Editor for Salary.com, quotes Lena Bottos, compensation market analyst for Salary.com, "When you take into account that it represents a 90-hour workweek, and doesn't even begin to factor in that they are on call 24 hours a day, it's not so large. Plus, stay-at-home moms get no benefits in terms of pension or 401(k)."[3]

Now that we realize our "Executive Status" in the home, how do we celebrate our achievements? Let's start with the basics. How about the simplicity of celebrating our abilities to get through those sleepless nights due to our youngsters' needs? How about the daily and hourly commitment we extend to our children to watch them blossom? How about focusing on all the amazing efforts and ways we help our children achieve success? Let's enter their world: children learn how to walk; accomplish new tasks, such as using scissors and solving a puzzle; learn how to ride a bike; how to catch with a mitt and how to hit the ball with a bat. When our kids reach these achievements, they are on top of the world. Let's celebrate that!

As busy moms, we have so many roles to fill. We strive for perfection as moms, spouses, sisters, daughters, friends, and professionals (if we're working outside of the home). Let's take a step back and think about how to celebrate all our roles, or at a minimum, how to nurture ourselves and celebrate our achievements as busy moms.

Questions to Ask Yourself

- How much time do I focus on my positive qualities?

- How much time do I focus on my mistakes?

- When was the last time I credited my own achievements as a busy mom?

- How do I celebrate those achievements?

- When was the last time I actually celebrated my achievements? If not, what has stopped me?

- Write down four ideas on how you can celebrate your achievements and actually calendar them.

Celebrating Your Own Special Self

- Treat yourself to a massage or a facial.
- Play your favorite music softly during a "quiet hour."
- Bake your beloved family recipe handed down through three generations.
- Give yourself a latte break after spending twenty-four hours nursing your child through the croup.

Singing Your Own Praises

- Congratulate yourself and your children when they achieve a new accomplishment, such as using the potty successfully for one consecutive week.
- Recognize the ways you support your school-age children when they achieve academic success.
- Recognize the ways you support your children when they achieve acts of kindness.

LIFE LESSON #2

Nurture Your "Whole" Self to Achieve Balance

Moving toward an inwardly simple life
is not about deprivation or denying
ourselves the things we want.
It's about things that no longer contribute
to the fullness of our lives. It's about creating
balance between our inner and outer lives.

Elaine St. James

✿ Blended and Balanced

We are a "blended" family. An interesting term, because it conjures up a vision of something smooth and deliciously creamy that always tastes great. Yet, my life as a "yours, mine, and ours" mom is challenging and hectic to say the least, with many lumps and bumps that can sometimes leave a sour taste in my mouth. Together we have seven children. The youngest, our daughter, and my three girls from a previous marriage live with us; my husband's two daughters and son visit every other weekend and alternate Wednesdays. Each child has a bed and space to call their own, which is "the good, the bad, and the ugly." As you can imagine, arguments erupt frequently over territory! I knew what I was getting into when we got married because we had already spent much time together as a family. *Love will conquer all,* I thought, but in the meantime, a truckload of patience and a few sacrifices are necessary, because there are more than one or two "just help me through another day" moments in my life. Coordinating ex-spouse visitations, PTA meetings, soccer practices, swim team meets, homework assignments, ferrying to and from schools, grocery shopping, at least one laundry load a day—sometimes two—trying to keep our home clean and tidy, participating in school fund-raisers that "pop" up sporadically and organizing a "social life." And I don't mean ours—I mean the kids!

I am proud of all that I juggle; working part-time from home while caring for our kids, preparing tasty meals, keeping the home running smoothly, and remaining cool, calm and collected under "fire"—even Dirty Harry would be proud. But lately the "Supermom" title has lost its luster, and I don't seem to stay quite so calm. Life has begun to feel like all work and no play, pushing me to the point of "overwhelmed." I find myself frequently resenting the many demands of my not so smoothly blended family, irritable at the slightest provocation and questioning my ability to cope. I have even considered talking to a therapist about some of these feelings, feelings that trigger guilt, which I am reluctant to share with my husband or any of my other "Supermom" friends.

On this particular Friday our seven-year-old woke up with a runny nose, complaining about her sore throat. "Beep-Beep-Beep." The thermometer signaled its readiness. It read 102°F. *Are we all going to get this?* I thought. *Just what I need—the whole family down with the flu!*

My husband headed to his office and my carpool partner collected the other three girls amid a flurry of teenage squabbling. An hour later my washing machine suffered "sudden cardiac death"—full to the brim with sudsy water and the day's first load. Ever hopeful, I pushed buttons and turned knobs while listening to the repair service tell me, "The earliest appointment is Monday between 8:00 and noon." *Didn't they realize I would be at least four loads behind by then?*

It was a little after 9:00 AM—my day had barely begun. Frustrated, I left the garage and began to mentally formulate the day's to-do list as I eyed the chaos of our hallway closet. *One of these days I'll get more organized,* I thought. Seeing my daughter's pajama-clad body disappear into the kitchen out of the corner of my eye, I climbed the stairs to take a shower and continued with my mental checklist.

I had a service appointment that I had scheduled for my car over a week ago because it was making a funny noise, but I still had to arrange for a rental. It was the end of the month and I needed to pay bills. My ten-year-old had asked for some help finishing a project that was due on Monday, and it was our turn to have all seven children, so I'd need to "supersize" my weekend grocery shopping before I picked everyone up from school.

I recalled my husband's words when he left that morning: "Love you!" And, "Oh, did I mention that I'm gonna have to work late tonight?" I thought back to the days when my own career made similar demands and sighed wistfully.

Maybe I should just get help and go back to work full-time.

The ringing telephone aroused me from the depths of my thoughts. I turned around and started back downstairs, trying to reach the phone before the answering machine picked up. "CRASH!" The sound of breaking glass, followed by a loud squeal, panicked me. Afraid my daughter had hurt herself, I abandoned all thoughts of answering the phone and quickly headed for the kitchen. As I changed direction I completely lost my balance and fell with a loud "THUD." My daughter, unscathed from her mishap, appeared in the kitchen doorway, the front of her pajamas colorfully splattered with orange juice. She wore a slightly bemused look on her face. "Mom, are you okay?" then she sneezed.

By now the machine was recording: ". . . so if there's any way you could help us out on Saturday morning, pleeeaaasssee call me back." Another volunteer mom had withdrawn her services from the bake sale at the school fund-raiser.

Still sprawled on the hallway floor, I shrieked at the answering machine, "YOU MUST BE KIDDING!"

The answering machine replied: "9:15 AM." I gathered my slightly bruised self up, not knowing whether to laugh or cry; maybe I really could use some therapy. The day was still young, but I wished it was over!

That was the day I decided to find someone to talk to

about my "Supermom Identity Complex," and the day I learned that I needed to slow down so I could keep my balance. Because, although I loved my family and wanted to excel as a mother, friend, and wife, I had to save a little something for myself, create a little elbow room and downtime between all the hustle and bustle where I could feel nurtured. The first time I spoke with the therapist, she asked, "What do you do for yourself?" When I realized the answer was "Nothing," I knew I needed to make some changes.

Since that fateful Friday I have begun to do a few things differently. I take a walk every day, if only around the block, so that I can be alone with my thoughts. Some sunny days I sit outside my favorite bakery with a cappuccino while I write my grocery list or finish a project for work. I've even started paying the older girls an allowance now, to help with a few chores around the house. And believe it or not I have signed up for an art class because painting has always been one of my lifelong dreams.

It's taken me awhile, but I finally feel that I have found a balance for my wonderful blended family and myself!

Gillian White

LIFE LESSON #2:

As busy moms, we are so busy taking care of others, we forget, feel guilty, or simply find it's impossible to take care of our "whole" self. Many of us feel that we are just trying to survive day to day, and anything else that we need to add to our schedule would throw us over the edge. The good news is that as our children grow up, our stressors change—so at least we get some variety!

We know that nourishing all the spokes on life's wheel—emotional, physical, mental, social, sexual, and spiritual—helps us achieve a well-balanced life. When we feed these spokes, we can evolve as "better moms." Yet we consistently put others first and rarely create time to nurture ourselves. The notion to nurture ourselves, such as trying to exercise, typically seems impossible. But the idea is balance and baby steps. We can keep our spokes interconnected. For example, when we are able to achieve even a twenty-minute workout, this can also benefit our mental, emotional, and spiritual spokes of life's wheel.

Emotional-Physical Balance

Many of us more than ever want to achieve a balanced life and know the beneficial outcome. Whether it's with our spouse, friends, or family, it is the experience of feeling connected on an emotional level that can nurture us through the hardest of times.

What else can we do? Scientific studies point out that a daily thirty-minute walk or other exercise can release natural endorphins to elevate our happiness and feelings of wellness. How can we busy moms fit this in? Let's use our creativity and walk a baby step in the right direction. When we hang out with our kids, we can turn on music and dance together or play games that involve jumping and running. For those of us who have a baby crawling on the floor, we can try some stretching exercises in close range. Even a subtle move such as good posture during a hectic dinner can help us feel better overall. And remember, adding deep breaths throughout the day will help us feel calmer and more composed.

And let's not forget the value of healthy eating habits and to schedule those important yearly medical checkups. When we protect our own health, we have more stamina to keep up with our busy lives and are able to provide the best to our families and ourselves both physically and emotionally.

Mental-Social Balance

Many of us, especially stay-at-home moms, feel isolated and yearn for a social life and intellectual stimulation. It's great to plan social time and playdates, but here's the reality: some of us juggle our days around feedings and naptimes, and sometimes just wing it in hopes that our child won't get too cranky. Then, when we're in the midst of our social hour, we can barely start a conversation of depth because it's hard to complete a sentence due to our kid's needing attention. What about social time over the phone when our kids are napping? Can we give up a precious hour to call a lifelong friend? Do we savor the reconnection or do we feel antsy halfway through our conversation? It's tough not to think about the fact that our toddler will soon wake up, the gas bill is due, and that cooking dinner is only forty-five minutes away. We feel like we can't win!

For those of us who have school-age kids, we're constantly running around driving them to and picking them up from school and taking them to and from extracurricular activities, not to mention the many ongoing errands we have when raising kids. So when we do have some spare time, we tend to try and get some personal things done versus hanging out with a friend to fulfill a social need. But somehow, we should find the time to meet our social needs, even if it's brief. Once we do, and especially if we're truly present, it can fill us up and make a tremendous difference. One way to connect with a friend and also get "stuff" done is to call a friend and simply say, "I only have about fifteen minutes, but I wanted to call and connect, even if it's only for a brief time." We may feel antsy the first few minutes, but eventually we'll relax. Making time to reach out to our friends can let some air out of the tires, providing us the opportunity to share our stories and laugh about life.

Intimate-Sexual Balance

Our sexual needs are also challenged, especially when parenting very young children. Breast-feeding moms are often depleted of sexual energy from low estrogen levels and fatigue. Most of us agree that our desire returns, but it does require work. The busiest moms agree that putting on fresh clothes and wearing some makeup can make a difference. And let's not discount our physical and emotional well-being to spur on intimacy. Exercise helps us feel good—body and mind. And when we connect on an emotional level with our spouse, it makes the difference in wanting to engage in other matters! Consider a weekly date night and start looking forward to those feelings of connectedness with the partner you love.

Spiritual Balance

Our spiritual side is very personal and individual. Whether it's praying to a higher power, participating in holiday rituals, lighting candles, building a fire, or watching a tree sway in the wind, spirituality helps to enhance our whole self. No matter how difficult it is to nurture this aspect of ourselves, life is constantly bringing new changes while we learn a new way to adapt. Watching our two-year-old discover a butterfly can itself be profoundly spiritual.

As busy moms, many of us feel that it is easier to just "let ourselves go," and before we know it, we may feel overweight, depressed, and overall in a terrible rut. Identifying the areas where we can make a difference in nurturing our "whole" self is progress. Taking baby steps to attain our goals in the areas that we have identified is naturally the next step. And how those small steps can make a difference! Something else to eventually look forward to when we watch our children becoming more independent is that we will be ready to enjoy the things we promised ourselves ages ago.

Also keep in mind: We can work so hard to achieve a balanced life by making efforts to nurture all aspects of ourselves. We may exercise, eat healthy foods, and make sure we get enough rest and time to unwind; however, if we truly have a medical condition, our strong efforts in all these areas may not make a difference. For example, if one is experiencing symptoms of depression, it is important to rule out a medical condition. Something as basic as the medical condition hypothyroidism could be responsible for these symptoms and could be ruled out by a simple blood test.

Although seeing a qualified physician to address our medical needs is of the utmost importance, in addition to this, many of us use the Internet to learn more about medical conditions to promote our health and well-being. When doing this, it is so important to know that we are reviewing information on credible sites. Below is an explanation of how to best "surf the Web" when looking for information.

Helping Moms Stay Afloat on the Internet

The Internet has become an important part of our lives and has completely changed the way we access information, helping us learn just about anything about everything. Yet, a website is no longer judged as valid and accurate based on its professional appearance. Today, a ten-year-old can design a website whose look can rival a website from some of the finest health institutions in the country. So how is a busy mom to know if the health information she is reading is correct? Online health information should never replace medical advice from your healthcare professional. Experts have developed certain criteria to use in evaluating whether a site is a good source of information. Think of these criteria as ingredients to a recipe for "surfing success": Start with authors who are *qualified* with appropriate credentials for the material being discussed. Add information that is based only on proven data and research. Eliminate any spoiled ingredients by stirring in updated information with the revised date clearly noted. Have a qualified panel of experts or board of directors sift through site content to ensure accuracy. Drain off and dispose of any sites where there is financial incentive or conflict of interest in the material being presented by any site owners, sponsors, or authors. Set aside and see if you can find the information elsewhere—if the content is accurate, it will appear on other *reputable* sites as well.

Still too busy to go through these steps to find what you are looking for? Then "surf" directly to government websites or websites of reputable academic institutions, many of which not only provide information, but also provide links to other valid and reliable sites.

Two examples of government websites that provide excellent information for women and girls are from the United States Department of Health and Human Services Office on Women's Health: www.womenshealth.gov and www.girlshealth.gov. Surfing that results in finding accurate information is educational and empowering, but remember to put down that "computer surfboard" and pick up your phone to speak with your own healthcare provider for medical advice specific to your unique health issues.

Cindy S. Moskovic, MSW
David Geffen School of Medicine at UCLA
University of California, Los Angeles

Begin taking baby steps with the following exercises:

- Write out past ways in which you were able to nurture your whole self before you had kids.

- Decide what you want now. How can you get there—even if it's on a much smaller scale?

- Complete the following:
  Ideas to achieve my emotional needs:

  Ideas to achieve my mental needs:

  Ideas to achieve my intimacy needs:

  Ideas to achieve my physical needs:

  Ideas to achieve my social needs:

  Ideas to achieve my spiritual/religious needs:

  How are all these spokes on my life's wheel interconnected?

Organizing Tips for Physical Balance

- Mark the calendar for your annual physical—we do not procrastinate in taking our kids to the doctor; we also need to consider our own health a priority.
- Plan a twenty-minute brisk walk three times a week while pushing your baby's stroller or take a walk with your school-age child.
- Consider stretching your body along with adding push-ups and sit-ups while hanging out with your kids—this also models the importance of exercise.
- Take some deep breaths during the day when your body says "time out."

Organizing Tips for Social Balance

- Schedule at least one to two playdates a week to refresh your emotional and social well-being.
- Three fifteen-minute phone calls a week with family and friends bring us closer to the people we love.

Organizing Tips for Intimate Balance

- Recognize that commitment to exercise can help you feel better about your body during intimacy.
- A "feel good" remedy may be as near as your closet—give the sweats a rest and wear your favorite outfit.
- Connect with your spouse for at least twenty minutes in the evening while the TV is off.

Organizing Tips for Spiritual Balance

- Take a few minutes during the day to enjoy the beauty of nature.
- Bringing religious rituals into your homes, even on a small scale, may fulfill a spiritual void.
- Ask your spouse to take care of the kids for an hour or so on the weekend, while you exercise, soak in the tub, or meet a friend for coffee.
- Meditate for fifteen minutes.

LIFE LESSON #3

Experience the Power of a Hug

A hug is a great gift—one size fits all,
and it's easy to exchange.

Author Unknown

❧ A Hug a Day

As a busy mother of eight children, my life can often be very hectic and filled with overwhelming amounts of stress. Surrounded with the daily responsibilities of taking care of such a large family, I have often found it hard to do even the simplest of things.

My life has been a truly blessed one. I have had eight children in just less than nine years. I have five handsome sons and three beautiful daughters. And like most mothers, I love my children more than anything in this world. There are times when this love is so overpowering, it brings me to tears. And although I know how much I love them, it wasn't till about a month ago that I realized that no matter how much you may love someone, no matter how filled your heart may be, you may not be showing that love at all.

It was a Wednesday afternoon. My three oldest children were just walking in from school. As I did every day, I began going through their backpacks, looking at their completed, graded work and seeing how much homework there was to complete that night. I pulled a large, folded-over piece of paper out of my oldest son's backpack. As I began looking it over, I realized that the previous week he had been named "Star Student of the Week." With this honor came the responsibility of filling out a paper telling all about himself. It was formatted like the front page of a newspaper. I slowly began to read it over.

He had described his family, his likes and dislikes, his own dreams for his future, and then, at the bottom, was a section titled, "One Thing I Could Change." It was here that I realized my love for my children may not have ever been expressed well enough.

There was only one small sentence written by the hand of my nine-year-old boy. It said, "I would change my Mommy's day so she would have more time to give me hugs."

My heart sank. I felt like I was losing my ability to breathe. This child, my firstborn, whom I loved more than my life itself, didn't think I hugged him enough! I quickly regained my composure and went about our normal afternoon routine. I tucked that paper away and didn't take it back out till all the children went to bed that night.

I sat and read it over and over and over. As the words fumbled through my brain, I began to realize something. My son was right! Although I do love my children, and I am overwhelmed and overjoyed with the gifts God has given me, I let the business and stress of my days take away from physically demonstrating my love to them. And with children, words alone are not quite enough. They need to be shown things. They need to feel things. They need their parents to love them with kisses and hugs every day, and not just before they leave in the morning and before they go to bed at night, as I had been doing. They need it all through the day and for no reason at all, except that you want to. And believe me, I do want to! I want to hug and kiss them every day, all day, never letting go. But I just never found the time. I let taking care of all the younger children and keeping my house clean and my laundry caught up take over my life.

These days are better. I make sure I hug and kiss all eight of my children a gazillion times every day. I will sneak up behind them and grab them up into the air, smothering them with my love and being smothered in return with their giggles. They are now beaming with joy and laughter, and the anticipation of when they will be "attacked" next. And although I never realized that they needed to be, my life and the lives of my children are so much brighter and happier.

So you see, it doesn't matter how much you love someone. It doesn't matter how good your intentions are. And it took the innocent words of my nine-year-old son to help teach me the most valuable of all the lessons in my life. "Although you may love someone so much you may be willing to die for that person, you have to always make sure you are living for them too!" And it brings a big smile to my face and to my heart to say that I finally am doing just that.

Veneta Leonard

✺

Life Lesson #3:

As busy moms, we get so caught up in our hectic lives that we sometimes forget the powerful effect of a simple hug. When giving or receiving a hug from our children, loved ones, or friends, we can experience the powerful act of nurturing going full circle.

We know that sometimes we feel worn-out and our kids may feel out of sorts. Let's turn these "blue days" around and ask our precious child for a great big hug; not just a meager one, but a huge, loving, arm-filling embrace. It's truly magical on both ends! And when children are hugged, they receive so many messages, such as feeling loved, valued, and connected.

Giving and getting a great big hug from a spouse, family member, friend, or child may help de-stress our bodies and release negative energy. When experiencing these loving embraces, without realizing it, we naturally tend to sigh and take a nice big breath, which also helps give us a sense of relief. It's a moment of shedding the hectic day and letting us know we are loved. It gives perspective.

Another area that may resonate with us is the following scenario: We feel like we're just about to fall apart and our spouse responds by giving us a big hug and asks, "What can I do to help?" Of course it doesn't always play out this way. Many would agree that men and women ask for help and affection in different ways: most men like to problem solve, whereas most women want to be heard (then problem solve). However, if a hug and to be heard is our first wish, then we may need to ask for it. Some spouses may figure it out by themselves; others may not. The intention of our spouses is that they do want to help, but sometimes they just don't know how. We need to tell our spouses what they can specifically do to help when this situation arises.

The simplicity of a hug sounds so basic, so simple. Yet too often, many days go barren without hugs or warmth. Although some would prefer not to receive hugs (it is important to honor and respect people's preferences), more often than not, whether giving or receiving, a hug can be a true blessing.

Let's remember the reason why we chose to start a family. Taking the time to demonstrate love to our family and friends is a powerful reminder that although being a busy mom presents us with many challenges, it's all worthwhile in the end.

Questions to Ask Yourself

- When was the last time you received a great big hug? How did it feel?

- When was the last time you initiated a great big hug? How do you think the other person felt?

- When growing up, were you hugged as a child? Did you have positive or negative experiences with hugs?

- Is giving or receiving a hug comfortable for you or does it feel awkward?

- If hugs are awkward for you, is there any person you are comfortable with so you can get that special hug in?

LIFE LESSON #4

Nurture Your Relationship
with Your Significant Other

Sticks and stones are hard on bones
Aimed with angry art,
Words can sting like anything
But silence breaks the heart.

Suzanne Nichols

✿ The Natural Cycle of Marriage

A friend asked me, "How many years have you and your husband been married?" I mentioned that we had just celebrated our six-year anniversary. "So, any anticipation of seven-year itching on the horizon?" Although it was a hectic time in life for both of us, my reply was, "No itching happening over here. We love each other more than ever!"

No more than a month later, the heat was on. I was eight months pregnant while trying to care for our twenty-three-month-old; we were in the process of buying a home, and my husband was working very long hours. Sparing greater details, to sum it up, we were experiencing some significant life stressors.

My husband and I always took pride in our communication skills throughout our marriage; we have always been there for one another and have been able to effectively work through our personal challenges and conflicts. So experiencing evenings of going to bed without knowing what to say to one another were some of the loneliest times I've ever had. Our frames of minds were at completely opposite ends. I was focused on how I was going to survive with two little ones and the need to get settled into a home with stability, while my husband was consumed with a very stressful job situation and conflicted about our decision to buy a new house.

About a month later, life continued to move forward with new hurdles and intensity. We moved into our new home, with my husband working long hours on moving day. A few weeks later, we were blessed with a second daughter and all the late-night feedings and diaper changes. Soon after, we received the devastating news that our precious dog had terminal cancer. My husband's work situation continued to escalate and he was traveling weeks on end. The stress in our lives was surmounting, and I was barely staying afloat with extreme sleep deprivation caring for our newborn. My husband and I acknowledged we were going through a tough time in our marriage and were quite unfamiliar with how estranged we felt from each other. We were tired. We weren't worried that our marriage was failing (fortunately we never did experience the "seven-year itch!"), however, we were at a loss how to get back to the loving place we were so used to living at with one another. A dear friend once said, "When both partners are depleted, it brings about the toughest of times."

I'm a realist. I know marriages have ups and downs. But I was not prepared for the place we had entered. Months went by and we were both more and more worn out. Then, one late night before bed, we happened to turn on a *Will and Grace* episode—the same one that had been on when I took a pregnancy test and found out we were pregnant with our first daughter. My husband cracked a joke about finally being able to see the complete episode. Somehow, that little moment put perspective on life. Maybe it was the beauty of remembering when we first learned we were pregnant. Maybe it was just laughing together. Whatever it was—we connected again. We stayed up late into the evening and shared how much both of us were stressed, and how much we missed each other.

From that night on, we both made efforts, albeit sometimes very small ones, to mend the places we were at odds with each other. My husband made significant effort trying to relate and understand where I was coming from during my days, and I did the same with him. I was also more conscientious with giving him space when getting home from his stressful workdays. And, beyond kids, work, a new home and receiving horrible news about our dog, we both made a commitment toward making our marriage a priority and just enjoying each other again. Over time, this consisted of making date nights for just the two of us, even if it was just grabbing a one-hour dinner over at the local BBQ joint. Although money was tight, we hired sitters. We knew taking time out to connect was an investment that would bring back great returns. Actually calendaring our date nights gave us something to look forward to with each other. We also made conscious efforts to be more affectionate, including giving each other foot massages while we read books to the kids. Most important, we made it a priority to take time to just talk and really listen to each other again, even if it was only for ten minutes before bedtime.

A handful of months later, our marriage was heading back "up" again. We started laughing more together, enjoyed each other's company, had a better appreciation for what the other one was going through, and our intimate life was sparking back up. And thank goodness for that!

Some people say that kids should always come first. My experience is that putting marriage on the same priority level as kids has a profound positive effect on the family as a whole. Now when we experience hard days, we make an extra effort to reach out. We've learned that showing love and compassion instead of isolating ourselves in our thoughts wins out. Sometimes when my husband walks into the house after work, and we're both feeling exhausted from our day—we've found that a ten-second hug, acknowledging that we're tired, expressing our love to one another, and making plans for dinner later in the week goes a long way. When my husband and I are supportive, nurturing and loving toward each other, it permeates throughout the house. Even our three-year-old gets a tremendous smile on her face whenever she sees her mommy and daddy giving each other loving embraces.

My husband and I recognize that there is no such thing as a "perfect" marriage; however, we believe ours is vibrant, healthy, and balanced because of our awareness that it must be nurtured and our commitment to do just that.

We've had tough times and know that the natural cycle of life will bring about more in our lifetime, but I thank God those rough times are with my husband. He is an incredible person, and I am deeply in love with him. He's my lover, my best friend, and the amazing father of my precious girls—taking time to nurture the relationship with my husband has become a priority.

Lynn Benson

LIFE LESSON #4:

Remember when we started out our lives with our spouses? We laughed together at the silly sitcoms and made popcorn for our date night. We had time to talk to each other and spent time planning a romantic evening or trip. We lived with few extravagances but we lived richly in love.

When we create blissful moments as described above to nurture the relationship with our significant others, we also attain the goal of nurturing ourselves. However, in our fast-paced society, many of us have difficulty slowing down to provide the emotional connection that can make a tremendous difference in our lives.

In addition to our busy lives taking the best from us, there is also a mind-set that may hinder us; that is, we have expectations that our spouses should equally reciprocate the nurturing efforts. Yes, it requires efforts from both, but a snapshot of reality usually depicts one partner as utterly depleted and exhausted. Fifty-fifty efforts are a great goal, but expect 60/40 or a 90/10 ratio as a more common phenomenon. When both spouses are worn-out, *that's when we really need to start rekindling our relationship to experience those blissful date nights again!*

The following scenario may be familiar to many of us. Our partners walk in at the end of the day and may have had a horrible time at work. They are irritable and do not want to talk about their day. One option is to get annoyed. We may feel frustrated by our spouse's mood; the other option is to give them a hug, a kiss and their own space. There's a good chance that if our significant others feel our love and acceptance for where they are, they will respond quicker when they've had a chance to unwind. Although we "should" avoid the expectation that our spouses will respond in a nurturing manner, more often than not, there's a good chance that they will.

As mentioned previously, our hope is that nurturing will be 50/50, but life doesn't always play out evenly. Weeks can go by, and as busy moms, we may feel neglected to the point where we want to explode. Yes, we've heard it all before—not to expect our partner to mind read and the importance of communicating our needs, but it's easier said than done. We each get so caught up in our own daily lives, we begin to think and communicate differently. But somehow we need to effectively communicate our needs. And the key is "effectively." Over time, whether we figure this out on our own or with the help of a therapist, we can find an effective approach that works well for our relationship, and it can elicit a more positive response.

Living the life of a busy mom without having a significant other to lean on can be harder than anyone can imagine. For those of us who are single, making it a priority to stay in touch with a close friend or relative to help promote that feeling of "connectedness" is important in achieving our efforts to nurture ourselves.

Ideas on Nurturing Your Relationship

In order to achieve the following, it is helpful to organize our daily lives with ways that include nurturing our relationships.

- Periodically send VERY brief and loving/romantic e-mails to each other.
- Periodically leave notes around the house with loving messages; for example, leave notes in the refrigerator (yes, *in* the refrigerator) or in the sock drawer for your spouse to find.
- Make time to give your significant other a hug.
- Take time to talk and connect for twenty minutes or so at night (no TV).
- Make an effort to kiss good night, even if you're arguing—it's not fun to go to bed angry.
- Cuddle when watching TV.
- Give your partner space to breathe and unwind after an exhausting day.
- Take turns preparing your favorite dinner once a week.
- And for heaven's sake, make a date night!!!! It's important to get a sitter. Reconnecting with your spouse is critical in rejuvenating your relationship.

LIFE LESSON #5

Make Time to Pamper Yourself (Guilt Free!)

There's no better way to energize your body,
mind and spirit than by taking care of yourself.

Stephanie Tourles

🌺 A Gift of Running

I am not the kind of runner who favors the quiet solitude of a solo run. If forced to run alone, I will. But to endure even one mile I need distractions like a Walkman, interesting scenery, and so on. Consequently I became quite discouraged when I moved to New York City and was forced to leave behind the faithful running partners I had been blessed with in my hometown of Atlanta. In Atlanta, I had any number of running buddies I could call upon no matter the hour or weather conditions. Even at ten o'clock on a rainy summer night I could persuade a friend to go for a quick three-mile run around town.

Naturally I anticipated finding the same type of running network in New York. Alas, this was not the case. While the population of New York far surpasses that of Atlanta, and the number of runners per square mile is no doubt staggering, in a year and a half I found no one who was a compatible running partner. New Yorkers keep strange hours and frantic paces. I found that my own life changed drastically with my move to the big city. So it became difficult to get myself on a regular running schedule, much less coordinate that schedule with another runner.

Fortunately I eventually connected with my current running partner. She has all the qualities you desire in a running partner. She is punctual, enthusiastic, works around my schedule, and is always at my beck and call. She even encourages me to go faster and will clap and cheer for me after I climb a steep hill or finish a really long run. She can be very difficult if I back out on a running date. She makes no attempt to veil her disappointment. It's that accountability that keeps me faithful on those days when the knees ache and the body is tired.

Now don't get me wrong—she is not perfect. She has her faults. She is guilty of annoyingly munching on a snack while we run. She chows down on a variety of finger foods. Much to my chagrin, she never gets winded. I can be huffing and puffing while she sings this week's favorite song at the top of her lungs. Perhaps the most unnerving habit she has is her uncanny knack of falling asleep around mile three or four.

You see, truth be told, I do the running and my partner mostly rides. My running partner is the nineteen-month-old daughter of my friend, a single mom. Thanks to the wonderful invention of the running stroller, I have someone to run with, and this toddler gets to go on an outdoor field trip. Being out of doors is a special treat for her, as her mom prefers the comforts of indoor living and ventures outside only when she is forced.

Being a single mom has been a real challenge for my

friend. She's had to say good-bye to the exciting New York nightlife. No more Broadway shows or cabaret acts. No more trying exotic restaurants or sipping drinks in swanky bars. Now it's cartoons, baby food, and diapers. It's been a dramatic change. She wouldn't trade it for the world, for she loves her young daughter, who has been a blessing in her life. This sweet baby is an unexpected blessing, but a blessing just the same.

Now that doesn't mean there aren't days when her eyes are glassy from too little sleep. And she's gone a whole week without washing her hair or shaving her legs! That never would have happened in her pre-baby life. She has, understandably, made that baby the number one priority in her life. So it took some persuading, but I finally convinced her to buy the running stroller. She would now tell you that it was the best baby purchase she has made, next to the bouncy seat. Sure, she only runs when trying to catch a bus, but the running stroller has given her the opportunity to enjoy a little alone time. While the baby and I are on one of our jogs around Central Park, my friend gets to pamper herself by reading a book, getting a manicure, meeting a friend for a cup of coffee, or sometimes just taking a much-treasured uninterrupted nap. She does this all guilt-free because she knows her baby is well taken care of and is actually on a fun field trip.

And I benefit too. Besides increasing the intensity of my

runs (have you tried pushing a twenty-pound baby up a hill?) and providing companionship, my new little friend has gifted me with so much more. She has taught me some invaluable lessons. When you run with a child, you are forced to see the world through that child's eyes. She becomes ecstatic when we pass a dog or a horse or even those nasty pigeons that populate our city. She calls them all "doggie," but we're working on "horse" and "bird." No matter how many times we've run past the carousel in Central Park, she still claps her hands and tries to sing along to the music. I'm guilty of not even noticing the carousel when I am alone. She has taught me to see the beauty in everyday things. The very act of running becomes a worshipful experience as I take in and marvel at all that God has created.

Now I must admit that I do miss the therapeutic talks I used to have with my adult running partners. Many a problem has been worked out on a long run. But there's a therapeutic nature to running with a child as well. I can't let my mind wander too much. I never know when we're going to have to retrieve a hair ribbon or make an unscheduled stop at the swings. My little partner dictates those diversions. Rather than dwelling on the day-to-day worries and concerns of my crazy and complicated life, I focus on getting a good workout and keeping my little friend both safe and entertained.

I believe that all three of us get something special out of our runs. They are so much more than just a field trip. I know I feel that I am giving both my friend and her baby a gift. My friend finally gets some time alone. It's time that truly belongs to her. She can shelf her responsibilities and focus on herself for a change. And she's a better mom for it. When we return from our outing, she is visibly relaxed, calm, and serene. She's ready to face whatever challenge or temper tantrum comes her way. She is renewed and refreshed! I get my workout, my little partner has a fun field trip, and all three of us feel the bond of a special friendship.

Sherry Bishop

Life Lesson #5:

Let's take a leisurely shower, manicure our nails, have lunch with a friend, or take a one-hour nap to rejuvenate ourselves. We know it's difficult to schedule time, but even the best of moms, who have an abundance of patience, wear down. It's time to replenish ourselves!

Some of us are fortunate to have family nearby, but this circumstance doesn't always lend itself to receiving the help we desperately need. It's imperative to consider hiring help, ideally two to three days per week to refresh our well-being. Even one day a week for a handful of hours will help nourish our mind. The art of nurturing ourselves also extends to busy moms who are working outside the home. An hour of exercise a couple days a week will bring relief on our overloaded days.

Many of us live on a tight budget. It's essential we reprioritize our spending habits to give ourselves that much-deserved break. Some swap playdates with a friend or neighbor who has similar-age children. While swapping dates can prove economical, the downside includes cancellations due to various reasons, such as children having colds or other unexpected life events. Hiring someone to come into our home, even for a half a day a week, is a much-needed gift that we moms truly deserve.

As busy moms, we want to do it all. When we are fortunate enough to get a break, many of us spend a great portion of the time feeling guilty, which completely defeats the purpose. Somehow we need to find that guilt-free place in our heart and soul, as we truly deserve to relish and cherish time for ourselves. This in itself can help significantly in rejuvenating our energy level so that we can give back more as a mother.

How often are we, busy moms, the last one to eat dinner, the last one to dress in the morning, or the last family member to catch up on sleep? We need to consider asking our spouses for more help. Sometimes we don't realize our passive-aggressive tendencies when we do not ask for a helping hand. Internal resentment can build up. When we communicate our need for more help to our spouses, it can make a tremendous difference.

For us busy moms who are fortunate to afford help, it would be great to celebrate our much-needed time for pampering. Too often it may feel like others are looking at us as if we have it so easy, and that we don't know what it's like to be a busy and utterly sleep-deprived mom. In reality, most of the moms who are fortunate enough to hire help are still up in the middle of the night, holding and nurturing their sick children and nursing them back to health. Yes, for those of us who are fortunate to hire help and who are not working outside the home, we may enjoy an easier time—no question about that—but we must not let others take away the hard work we do as busy moms and the fact that we get depleted too.

Consider this: when we continue to take more and more funds out of our bank account without adding a drop of money, our account becomes depleted, then empty. That's how our body operates. By investing in our well-being, the dividends will pay off handsomely toward our happiness and contentment. And what a profound difference our well-being can make on our entire family.

Questions to Ask Yourself

- When's the last time you pampered yourself?

- If you experience guilt, how did that penetrate into your life?

- What kind of pampering works best for you?

- How can you create a "time to pamper" yourself?

Food for Thought

Consider adding a nap to your list, if at all possible. Sleep deprivation is tougher on us than most realize. We must make efforts to get caught up on our sleep. It's a basic necessity to optimize our daily functioning.

Organizing Tips to Pamper Yourself

- When your kids take their naps, stretch out on the couch, even if you don't fall asleep.
- Add your favorite magazine or newspaper to the weekly grocery list.
- Ask your partner to take a turn giving the children's baths while you watch TV or phone a long-time friend.
- Spend extra time in the shower using your favorite soap.
- Take a break and go to a movie, shopping, or whatever your heart desires.

LIFE LESSON #6

Create Boundaries and Be Okay with Saying "No"

Conquering any difficulty always gives one a
secret joy, for it means pushing back a
boundary-line and adding to one's liberty.

Henri Frederic Amiel

✿ Juggling Act

On this particular November morning, I left for school early. My kindergarten students were having a special program, and I wanted to make sure everything was ready. As I drove to school, I checked all the mental lists I'd been making for weeks. Besides worrying about the program and working on lesson plans every evening, I was busy with my family and a host of volunteer activities. I had three different carpools, PTA meetings, and served on various community and school committees. My husband did as much as he could around the house, but he worked long hours, so I had to manage the grocery shopping, the laundry, the meals, helping the kids with their homework, and driving them to and from their after-school activities. Still, whenever I was asked to help out at a rummage sale at school or sell tickets for a local charity event, I always agreed. I knew I'd developed a reputation as someone who couldn't say "no," but I enjoyed doing these things; I felt helpful and useful. Sometimes—like now, as I inched along at a frustratingly slow crawl through the morning rush-hour traffic, anxious about all the things I had to do—I felt as though I were onstage, juggling flaming torches. But still, I always managed, and I was confident that as long as I kept things organized, I'd be able to stay in control and everything would get done.

Midway through the morning, the children gathered at the table for their snack. I finished pouring apple juice into sixteen little paper cups and then left my teacher's aide in charge while I went to the office to get the tape recorder we would need for the next class activity. The door of the media closet in the office was stuck, and as I tugged at it, I felt an ache in both of my shoulders. When I crouched down to move a large box out of the way, I was surprised to find that it was heavier than I'd expected, and I lost my balance, and suddenly, I was sprawled on the floor. I immediately started giggling, both at my clumsiness—I've always been one of those people with "two left feet"—and at my relief that the secretary happened to be out of the room at the moment, so I was spared that embarrassment. But my laughter quickly stopped as I struggled to get to my feet and realized with shock that I couldn't get up. I knew that nothing was broken, so it wasn't from the fall; it was just that I didn't have the strength to pull myself up.

At that moment, the secretary returned, and by now I was glad to see her. "Are you alright? What happened?" she exclaimed, helping me up.

"I lost my balance, but I'm OK," I reassured her, although I wasn't at all sure that was true.

As I carried the tape recorder back to my classroom, I couldn't help but remember all the little nagging worries I'd been having for several weeks, and the incidents that provoked them: the day I'd stumbled in a parking lot and fallen flat on my face, bruising my cheek; the pain in my legs when I sat on the floor with the children; and the increasing difficulty I was having getting up out of the little chairs in the classroom. At first, I'd figured I was just out of shape, but now I wasn't so sure. Something was wrong, and I was scared.

As soon as I got home, I called my doctor. She sent me for blood tests and X-rays, and a few days later, I had an answer: I had an autoimmune disorder that caused muscle pain and extreme weakness. It could be treated, the doctor told me, but it would probably take several months.

I started treatment immediately, but as the doctor had warned me, things got worse before they got better. By Thanksgiving, I could barely walk, and I had to take a leave of absence from my job. My muscles were so stiff and sore that my husband had to help me get dressed every morning before he left for work, and help me in and out of the bathtub at night. I couldn't drive since I didn't have the strength to turn the steering wheel, so the other carpool mothers took over, and my sixteen-year-old daughter, who had recently gotten her driver's license, did the grocery shopping.

Even though I was tired and achy all the time, I spent a few hours on the computer every day, compiling curriculum ideas and detailed lesson plans for the substitute teacher who had taken over my class. Even though I couldn't go to work, the "superwoman" in me felt compelled to fax my lesson plans to the school every day.

As it turned out, my sense of control was just an illusion. When I called the school one day to talk to the principal, I found out that the substitute wasn't using the lesson plans I'd so carefully prepared; she was making her own. I noticed other things slipping away from me too: since my daughter was doing the grocery shopping, and my husband was cooking, I wasn't in charge of what we ate for dinner. The other mothers in the carpool rearranged the driving schedule. The PTA came up with a whole new fund-raising program. And I had no say in any of it.

At first, I was unhappy and uneasy; I felt anxious about the things I wasn't doing, guilty that I wasn't doing them, and even a little hurt that I wasn't involved. But gradually, I started seeing things in a different light.

One day, a large envelope arrived in the mail. Inside were pictures of the rain forest that my students had constructed in the classroom, under the guidance of the substitute teacher. It was completely different from the way I would have done it—and it was fantastic. Later, the president of the PTA called to tell me about the new fund-raising program, and I told her it was a terrific idea. And that night, my husband and the kids made a meat loaf for dinner, with a spicy sauce made from a "secret" recipe. It was delicious.

After dinner, as my husband did the dishes and the kids took out their homework, I realized that terrific things were happening right there in my own house, too. My having to let go allowed my children to try just a little harder, and do just a little more than they'd thought they could do. And I realized I had to trust other people to be competent, to do a good job, even if it wasn't exactly the way I would have done it.

It was a long winter, but I slowly regained my strength, and by March, I was able to return to my job, resume driving the carpools and even go to PTA meetings. But I decided that that was where I'd draw the line. No new committees, no additional obligations. In part, I knew that I needed to say "no" sometimes and be realistic about how many flaming torches I could really juggle, just to maintain my own health. But I also knew that I wasn't just being selfish and letting someone else pick up the slack. My letting go didn't leave a void; it allowed others to rise to the challenge, to reach out and grab one or two of the flaming torches, and share the spotlight and the satisfaction of a job well done.

Phyllis Nutkis

LIFE LESSON #6:

Women are often gifted nurturers. We have a genuine desire to please and take care of others. As busy moms, we also tend to feel that we "should" take care of everyone around us that is in need. As a result, we spread ourselves so thin that many of us find that there isn't enough of "us" to go around. We try to be the best wife possible and the most amazing mom on earth. We want to help out relatives and friends who are in need and not let them down, and if working outside the home, we expect ourselves to perform at the top of our game. Wow! That's a lot for one woman. Instead of beating ourselves up, let's give ourselves LOTS of credit for a "job well done." And let's also give ourselves LOTS of credit when we become secure with saying "no."

When can we actually say "no"? For starters, let's organize our thoughts and do a self-evaluation. It would help to think about what is working versus not working for us in our lives. We need to ask ourselves, "How many times in my day do I agree to do something and wish I had not?" If we are able to actually say "no," how many of us spend time feeling guilty about it? So often we say "yes" to the point that we can lose ourselves in the process.

Creating boundaries to identify what will work for us is

a critical achievement. Then, once we actually can say "no" to someone, a significant goal to reach is to let ourselves say "no" without feeling guilty. Also, how often do many of us feel we must explain to others why we are unable to say "yes"? The truth is, it's really no one's business. Simply stating, "It's not going to work out for me to attend . . . " is really all that's necessary. Nothing more! Just because other moms are able to attend everything under the sun—and yes, we absolutely appreciate all the hard work they do put in—it doesn't mean we must do the same. The reality is, we all have different strengths, different energy levels, and different life stressors; therefore, we need to figure out what's really going to work out best for ourselves. Saying "yes" to something because we are genuinely okay doing it tends to feel a whole lot better.

> Saying "no" can test our strength. That's when we need to "mother" ourselves.

Questions to Ask Yourself
- Do I have a hard time saying "no" to others?

- Do I feel I have overloaded my plate?

- Do I continuously feel like I'm letting others down?

- How much of the day do I feel guilty?

- How often do I say "yes" when I really wish I had said "no"?

- Which people can I say "no" to? Why do I think this is?

- If I have a difficult time saying "no," write out why I think this is so.

- To create clear boundaries, write out which areas work for me in my life and which do not.

Write goals of how I can achieve clear boundaries in my life and what steps I can take to get there.

"I'll come out and play in a minute.
I'm having a teachable moment."

TAKE CHARGE OF YOUR PARENTING STYLE/PHILOSOPHY

*My father didn't tell me how to live;
he lived, and let me watch him do it.*

Clarence Budinton Kelland

LIFE LESSON #1

Evaluate and Clearly Define Your Parenting Philosophy

The art of mothering is to teach
the art of living to children.

Elaine Heffner

❧ When Life Gives You Lemons

The heat index is up over 100°F. There is no breeze and no shade on the makeshift lemonade and cookie stand where Haley sits and waits for her first customer. Lined on rickety TV trays in front of her are bags marked in her seven-year-old handwriting "Chocolate Chip," "Pecan Raisin," and "Oatmeal." I'm sitting on the tailgate of our van reading a magazine and thinking what a great learning experience this will be. Her first potential customer is a conservative blue sedan. I sit back, ready to watch my young entrepreneur in action. Haley sees it too and straightens up in her folding chair, adjusts the rows of cookies on the trays in front of her, and beams a smile at the driver who smiles back and drives on.

This is good. I think. *It shouldn't come too easily for her.* I can't see her face and start to holler something reassuring to her, but before I can come up with anything, I see a minivan heading her way. *Another parent. They'll stop.* I watch Haley straighten herself again. The young mother in the van smiles, waves, and she too drives on. Haley's shoulders slump. Three more cars pass. I pretend to read my magazine.

I don't see the next car. I hear it—an earth-shattering, rap beat exploding from a low-riding truck. *This is perfect, I think. This kid is young enough to remember cutting the neighbor's grass for spending money. He can relate to another kid sitting in the sun trying to make a few bucks off cookies and lemonade. He'll stop and Haley will have learned how to be patient and wait for what she wants.* I see the teenager glance over quickly, then speed off, his tires squealing on the pavement. I guess it's not cool to stop and buy lemonade when you're seventeen.

Haley looks back at me with a pained expression. I smile reassuringly for a second then force myself to glance back to my magazine. *She needs to learn this on her own. I tell myself, I have to let her experience disappointment without me always cushioning the blow.*

But when five more cars pass, I start to get mad! *What's wrong with these people? Weren't they ever kids themselves?* Another car passes. *Didn't they ever sit at a lemonade stand in the heat waiting for someone to stop and buy their wares?* Two more cars. *This is breaking my heart! How can they drive past her hopeful face without stopping?*

Realizing Haley is looking back at me, I put down my magazine and walk to her. "Why isn't anybody stopping, Mom?" She isn't sad or upset, just confused. "This isn't the way you thought it would be, huh?" Is all I can come up with. I want to say, *Because they're jerks, honey. That's why.*

Feeling helpless, I watch another car approach. I wonder if I stare hard enough at his front tire if he'd have a blowout and have to stop. *I've never passed by a kid at a lemonade stand in my life,* I'm thinking, *even in my college days when I had to scrape together pennies off the floorboard*—but when I look up, I see Haley confidently pouring lemonade and reciting her cookie menu for a middle-aged man. "I have chocolate chip, raisin pecan, and oatmeal. The oatmeal are the best." Listen to my articulate little girl.

A group of kids is running up the street, money in their fists. A smaller group hollers for them to "Wait up!" Suddenly, Haley's stand is swarming with children shouting orders and reaching for bags of cookies. I hurry up to her and ask if she needs help. "No, Mom. I think I can handle it." She's counting out loud, pouring lemonade, and distributing cookies, calm and self-assured. Look at my girl go!

Another van stops and more kids are running her way. Haley can't resist flashing a smile back at me. When she proposed this project, I figured it would provide her with a math lesson and something to do for a summer afternoon. I hadn't realized how much she'd learn about patience and determination. I hadn't realized how much I'd learn about giving her the freedom to learn it on her own.

Mimi Greenwood Knight

LIFE LESSON #1:

Remember the last time our children decided to stay up beyond their usual bedtime? Before we could even say, "It's bedtime," they exclaimed, "Daddy said we can stay up!" Children can truly benefit when their parents are clear about their parenting philosophies, especially when both parents are on the "same page." When parents are not in sync with each other, children can pick up on these differences and may align themselves with one of their parents. To prevent this, we need to support each other and present a united front. With a team effort, there are a number of positive outcomes, such as fewer tantrums from our kids, which can make family time more enjoyable. Decreased outbursts also mean a better chance of arriving to places on time. And less tantrums can also help us achieve our optimal levels of efficiency, day-to-day functioning, and ability to stay organized during very hectic days. Most of all, implementing the most positive parenting philosophy possible in conjunction with one another can help promote all-around healthier and well-balanced children.

Examples of areas to help define parenting philosophies with our children may include the choice of words we use, how we "model" for our kids, the style of discipline we use, the consistent limits we set, and the type of food we allow our children to eat. For example, if one parent feels strongly about keeping junk food away from the kids, and the other parent loves cupcakes, then a compromise could be that every Saturday is the day the family enjoys their favorite dessert. Of course, it's natural to disagree periodically about which direction to go with our philosophies; this is the time to make a commitment to compromise.

Another important aspect to think about is how we may disagree with each other when we are actively parenting our children. One of us may be quick to correct the other parent in front of our children; however, when possible, this would be better to do in private. This way we as parents can exhibit our united front. Okay, easier said than done. After all, arriving at the place to show our united front is a task in itself, but it's well worth the effort!

Once we evaluate, define, and implement our parenting philosophy, it can make a tremendous difference with our confidence. It gives us greater ability to follow through, maintain consistency, set limits, and model effective communication skills, which children desperately need.

Keep in mind, the more we learn, the more we realize we don't know! Wouldn't it be great if it was the other way around? Therefore, it makes sense that we may need to readjust our parenting philosophy as time goes on. Also, as children reach different and new developmental phases, certain approaches that may have worked previously may need altering. Although children may have difficulty adjusting to a new style and approach initially, in time there is a high probability that they will adjust, and the whole household will truly benefit from it.

Exercise to Complete

- Are you and your spouse clear on your parenting philosophy? Do you convey a "united front" to your children?

- If you are both clear on your parenting philosophy, how would you sum it up in a brief paragraph?

- If not, write down your philosophy and ask your partner to do the same.

- Where do you see consistency? Where do you differ?

- After discussing it, write down a parenting philosophy on which you can both agree.

Ideas to Promote Our Parenting Style/Philosophy

- If we want our children to possess good manners, let's mirror the habits we want them to use.
- Children benefit and know their parameters when we provide consistent limit setting.
- Emotionally charged arguments in front of our children can weaken the family unit. Making a commitment to problem solve in an effective and calm manner can help develop our kids' interpersonal skills.

LIFE LESSON #2

Practice Consistency

It's not what you leave to your children,
it's what you leave in your children.

Unknown

❧ Picking Your Battles

"NO PANTS! I want to wear my pajamas!" My three-year-old was filled with righteous indignation over my suggestion that it was time to get on a shirt and pants for preschool.

His arms were folded over his chest, and his lip jutted out in defiance. Irritated and about to run late, I dug in my heels. "Ez, you have to wear clothes to school."

"I *am* wearing clothes!" The child even stomped his foot at that statement. But he did have a point. It wasn't like he wanted to go flouncing off to school in his birthday suit, although that scenario was certainly possible. *Let's cross that bridge when we come to it,* I figured, hoping fervently we wouldn't.

Faced with this flannel-clad bundle of opposition and with about five minutes to put out this fire—or fuel it—I made a choice to let this one go.

"Ez, you may not talk to me like that, but you may wear your Thomas the Tank Engine jammies if you ask nicely." Stunned that he could actually be allowed to do so, Ezra acquiesced. He unfolded his arms, un-pouted his lower lip, and then asked nicely if he could please wear his pajamas to school.

The thought flitted through my mind that my mother never, under any circumstances, would have allowed her little child to attend school or any other public function wearing pajamas. She would have as soon burned her bra in a front-yard bonfire and declared herself a patriot of the women's liberation movement.

But I, semiliberated and wearing a bra, picked a battle at that moment. Or rather, I picked "no" on fighting that particular battle. Why? Well, it's preschool, not the SATs. You know, finger painting and cookie baking, an unstructured, winsome place where whimsy and wonder abound. I knew he would be sufficiently warm and decently clothed, and also that his whimsical teachers wouldn't blink an eye over Ezra's one-man pajama day. (Indeed, Miss Susan and Miss Catherine celebrated his entrance with great fanfare and made a big fuss over how silly and funny and wonderful Ezra was to wear his pajamas to school!)

Motherhood is crammed with opportunities to pick a battle or to step out of the ring. I could have forcibly stripped Ezra of his pajamas and then wrestled him into some school clothes. Or maybe I could have threatened him with consequences. The thing is, I knew it would be a huge ordeal to force him to do what he so clearly didn't want to do. Was it easier to let him attend class wearing his jammies? Absolutely.

The child has a will so steely it boggles my mind. We could be in the ring all day long at times, duking it out over some disagreement or other. But if I turn every misdemeanor into a felony, I'll lose my maternal authority and probably my mind. Shaping and guiding a preschooler's moral character will be a long, hard slog, so I've learned to save my energy for the lessons he really has to learn.

Lorilee Craker

Life Lesson #2:

Many of us are too exhausted to practice consistency, which in turn makes the efforts that we have tried to establish go down the tubes. Nevertheless, it's worth trying it again to make it happen. Implementing consistency is exhausting in the beginning, but it can make a tremendous difference in the long run. However, there is a caveat to achieving consistency; that is, we must choose our battles. After we have identified our parenting philosophy, we need to zero in on what really matters—think about the bigger things and not sweat the small stuff. There is always the importance of balance: to give our children consistent guidance, and also give them enough space so that we are not overly protective, which enables our kids to build their independence and confidence.

The developmental age of the child is also very important to take into account. As we know, two- and three-year-olds and teenagers express a huge degree of power struggles. Therefore, these are prime periods where it can make a profound difference to choose our battles and remain consistent with what we have determined to be important in limit setting. For example, as parents we may desperately want our teenagers to dress more "tidy." And yes, the trends today are unbelievable, but we may choose to be a bit more lenient in this area and remain firm with them about completing their homework. When our kids are in their phases of power struggles, we will be entrenched with choosing our battles—if not daily, hourly—especially when they're teenagers!

Let's also think about the benefit of making room for special allowances. When we provide this, it's especially important to explain to our child why a special circumstance is permissible. This shows and models flexibility.

Another area to consider is to allow ourselves to admit when we make a mistake and say we are sorry to our kids. This is an example of how we can model an important aspect of integrity to our children. And what a relief—to allow ourselves space—to not be perfect.

An additional factor that can make a tremendous difference for our children is to provide consistency and structure within their daily routine. When we offer structure with flexibility, it helps our children thrive. It also helps them feel more secure and to know what to expect. And we as adults typically benefit from this very same concept.

Implementing consistency for children may be very challenging at first. Kids may challenge it and things may get worse before they get better; however, in time we'll be glad we did it! Just remember to try and focus on effectively communicating with your children as you employ consistency. Children understanding the reason behind our rules or actions can go a long way!

Questions to Ask Yourself

- How consistent were my parents with me?

- Am I consistent with my child in the areas that I believe are important? If not, in what areas do I need to ensure more consistency?

- Is my spouse consistent with our child in the areas that we believe are important? If not, in what areas do we need to implement more consistency?

Practicing Consistency—Tips

- When employing consistent limit setting, we should always consider the developmental age of our children.
- The more confident we are with our parenting philosophy, the easier it is to be consistent.

LIFE LESSON #3

Remember to Follow Through

*Your children will see what you're all about
by what you live rather than what you say.*

Wayne Dyer

🌺 Three Red Xs

Three red Xs took up half the page on the note that my Nicholas, age eight, brought home from school last year. Arrows pointed to the line that said, "Does not play nicely with others." At the bottom, his very nice first-year teacher wrote, "Other than the above issue, Nicholas is a joy to teach!! Can we schedule a conference for TOMORROW?"

All the people in the past who told me I should put my child in preschool so he could learn to get along with others came rushing back to me. *Was he kicking little Johnny? Or pulling Susie's hair? Was he stealing toys? Or heaven forbid, not sharing?*

After phone conversations with my mom and my best friend, who both assured me it was probably not a big deal, I called her.

"Nicholas is having twenty-minute crying jags when he doesn't win a game we are playing in class," his teacher told me.

"He is?" I asked, perplexed at this turn of events. My son always won at home, so how would I know how he would react? Every parenting book in my home said that children should feel special and accepted. I followed this advice to the letter, with only three red Xs to show for it. I mentally consigned Dr. Spock and his entire ilk to the landfill.

"Do you think you could work on this at home? Winning isn't everything," she reminded me.

We had our first official game night that evening. Before I pulled the game out of the box, all four children were fussing over who would go first. I could still visualize the teacher's note.

"I get to take it out of the box!"

"I get to sit by Mama!"

How would we ever get through the first game? At the rate we were going, the hour would pass and the game would still be sitting on the table unopened.

If I was going to help Nicholas learn how to play well with others, I would need to act as a referee. "We are going to read the rules first," I told my kids. I took the box from the two red-faced children engaged in a tug of war, yellow and blue gingerbread men pieces flying. "In order to play any game, every player must know how to play."

Thankfully, Candy Land's "official game play instructions" included that the youngest child should go first. I imagine the game creators added that little jewel after listening to much howling from their test subjects over this issue. My kids settled down and we started this game on a high note.

Then one of those Xs reared its head. Two minutes into the game, Nicholas had a breakdown: "Everyone else has moved two color spaces. I've only moved one colored space." He screamed loud enough to wake the neighbor, who did not wake up when a tree from Hurricane Katrina slammed into her roof.

I put on my best Super Nanny persona and explained to him that most games are about chance and that everyone could not move two spaces. Nicholas vented his frustrations, "I hate this game!" I let him know that all games, including Candy Land, come with rules. And everyone who plays a game needs to know how to play fairly.

Fifteen cry fests, eight time-outs, one hundred and twelve reminders that game play is not about winning, and two hours later, we managed to complete the game.

The situation was dire, but I was determined. "Talks at inappropriate times" might be okay, but "does not play nicely with others" was not. I knew I could guide Nicholas and that he would gradually see the correct way to play with others, but I had to dig in my heels and not give in to him.

Family game night turned into every night. We progressed to ten cry fests and three time-outs in one week. Each time we played Nicholas got better, but I still needed to help him realize that playing a game was not only about winning, but learning how to play well with others. By the end of week two, all the kids started to relax and enjoy playing the game—even I looked forward to it—and one month later, no one cried over losing. The children even learned to congratulate the winner with "good job" and a pat on the back.

The star on the Christmas tree occurred at the end of the year when I again received a note from Nick's teacher, this time praising his skills at playing nicely with others. "He even helps children who are not so good at it," she added near the bottom.

A year and a half later, we still have game night. The phones and TV turned off, on our rickety table that the marbles from Chinese checkers roll off of, we sit together. We laugh, learn, and play. I never thought that three red Xs could teach our family so much.

Tiffany Todd-Fitch

LIFE LESSON #3:

Once we have identified our parenting philosophy, implementing the basics to follow through with our children can make a profound difference in a number of areas. For example, the simplicity of following through when we tell our child that we are going to do something can help build the foundation of trust. It's also imperative to follow through when giving consequences; otherwise, our efforts become meaningless.

When we effectively communicate the rules and boundaries that we establish, our children will have clear guidelines to follow. But when our kids break the rules, they are entitled to know the consequences ahead of time so they will not feel caught off guard. For example, if a rule exists that our child only gets dessert after she eats her vegetables at dinner, then let's put a positive spin on our approach. Remind her that when she finishes her vegetables, she can enjoy dessert, versus the negative approach, "You won't get your dessert if you don't eat your vegetables." Sometimes rephrasing a request with a positive spin can make all the difference. If our children choose not to eat their vegetables in this scenario, it is especially important to follow through and not give in with dessert.

Most would agree that it is difficult to follow through when our children begin to throw a tantrum, especially in public! Don't we just love it when this happens? When this occurs, it may seem easier to relax the rules so the problem just goes away. In addition, it's hard to see our children upset and distressed. But, as we all know, not following through sets up a pattern for our children to act out because ultimately they know they will get their way.

Another parenting "trap" in which we may occasionally find ourselves is suggesting a consequence that we actually do not intend to carry out. For instance, after trying a positive approach, we may find ourselves saying, "We're not going to the birthday party if you don't clean up your mess." If that consequence won't actually happen, let's not even mention it. And yes, easier said than done!

As previously pointed out, we want to focus on a positive approach as much as possible. And, as we know, positive reinforcement can go a long way. Although we dearly love our children, at various times we may have difficulty finding pleasant behaviors within them. When we experience this situation, it's helpful to focus on "catching" our children when they exhibit positive behaviors. When they play well, even for a moment, catch them "in the act" and praise them. Furthermore, when we tell our children, "You did a great job listening today," and "You will be getting a special treat at the end of the day," we must remember that it may not seem like a big deal to us if we forget, but in their world, it can mean everything. Even following through with the smallest of acts can have a big impact.

The benefit from following through with our children, in addition to making a difference regarding our child's self-esteem, it can also certainly make our days much smoother when living the life of a busy mom.

Organizing Tips to Follow Through with Children

Mental Notes for Our To-Do List:

- If we tell our children we will take a certain action or buy them a special item, we should consider writing our promise on the calendar OR put a sticky note on the fridge to remind ourselves to follow through.
- If we tell our children they're not going to get to play with the Legos for the next two days because they refused to clean them up, it may be helpful to write a note to remind ourselves OR place the Legos out of sight for two days.

LIFE LESSON #4

Set Limits

Live so that when your children think of
fairness and integrity, they think of you.

H. Jackson Brown

🌺 A Lesson in Compromise

Parenting came to me so naturally—at least it did before the children were actually born. Back then, when I imagined setting a limit for my kids, it was like an object framed behind glass: There it is! The limit I'm setting! Isn't it fine? I imagined "No galloping with the bread knife!" and "That's enough black jelly beans for one day!" I felt very clear and capable, there in my imagination. And I was right, in a way, because sometimes it's so easy. Not the aftermath, necessarily—where your toddler lies on the sidewalk pounding her little fists and rain boots into the asphalt, keening and groaning because you wouldn't let her dart out in front of a truck—but the limit itself: "You can't run out into the street." There's really no gray area there. No wheeling and dealing. No room for compromise.

But then, more often than not, the clear light of health and safety fogs over with negotiation. Limit setting starts being less about what the kids *do* and more and more about how they act, how they are—and, it almost goes without saying, how you are. Because ultimately how you set it— how consistent and kind you are, for instance—will be as important as the actual limit itself. It hardly needs saying that these interactions we have with our kids will (we hope) serve more as guiding lights than blindfolds as they find their way through life's maze of conflict and compromise. And it takes true patience. Not the kind that obliges you to sit still beneath a napping child or frost 200 cupcakes in a single afternoon (no problem), but the kind of patience that requires you to maintain respectful attention while other people express ideas vastly different from yours about how things in the world should be. And boy, am I not patient.

Like last night, when we had some friends over, and the three big kids performed a magic show after dinner. These are Ben's magic tricks, so he knows them well and has developed a flourishing kind of showmanship to boot, which means that his friends' bumbling around the magnetic multiplying dice or stuttering over their *Alacazam* really kind of annoys him. And so he was inclined to become frantic, to be a little bit bossy with them—albeit in his fairly gentle way—but I started to feel about Ben's impatience, well, impatient. And also something else— something like *embarrassed* that my kid was bossing around my friends' kids. All very minor stuff in most ways, I realize, nothing you'd need to make an after-school special about, but the babies were sobbing, and the grown-ups were zipping their jackets up, and the evening desperately needed to end, and when Ben wanted to do "one last" magic trick after the "very last" one, I said no. And Ben fell apart.

I don't know how to explain what I regret, because it's nothing that I've actually described. It was right to coach Ben away from bossiness; it was right to say no to that last trick. These were perfectly appropriate limits. But it was the way that I did these things, the way that I communicated disappointment or anger—I could feel it in my face, in the hardness of my jaw—when Ben was just being a kid, learning the ropes even as he's climbing them, just like the rest of us. I think I just wished that I'd been kinder. I wished I'd been just as firm, yet also just as firmly *on his side:* a shining example of how to act even during the inevitable struggles and conflicts, even during the compromises.

More patient. I am wrestling with it. Impatience is the sweaty hulking shape rolling around on the mat with me. Every morning I wake up and vow to be more patient, and some days I succeed. And so many days I don't. This night, the magic show night, it was a little of each: that lovely little Ben got miserably ready for bed while I searched myself for kindness, patting at all the empty pockets of my soul. And at last I said to him, "That happens to grown-ups too—when it's so hard to let other people do things the way they want to. It happens to me all the time, and it's the most frustrating thing—trying to compromise." And Ben's face and body softened with relief; he relaxed, chatted with me about his frustration with the other kids, his anger when I wouldn't let him do his last trick. It took an almost physical act of strength to do it, but I did: hand over hand, concentrating like my life depended on it, I hauled myself out of anger and into compassion.

And maybe next time I'll start there in the first place.

Catherine Newman

LIFE LESSON #4:

At times, children seem to enjoy testing our "patience quotient." But do not despair; children feel safer when parents provide firm limits, and it can help them experience a higher degree of self-esteem. If parents do not provide boundaries, children can feel "out of control." Also, engaging in appropriate limit setting can make a big difference for busy moms; the more effective we are with our parenting, the more effective we will be going through each and every day.

As adults, we live in a world filled with rules and restrictions. This gives us boundaries of what is okay and limits on how we need to carry out our lives. We must abide by the laws our judicial system has created; otherwise, we will be faced with the consequences. Also, in the workforce, many companies provide policy manuals for employees.

These examples may be a bit of a stretch, but by the same principle, children need similar structure. At a young age, implementing limit setting can set the tone to help children evolve and prepare for their lives ahead.

The manner of how we set limits for our children is very important, and it can be approached in a number of positive ways. The more confident we are as parents in providing limits and boundaries, the more likely our children will sense our confidence, which can make a difference in how they respond to us. Of course, we need to keep perspective. Just as our confidence as a parent is rocketing, our children exhibit a new behavior that throws us for a loop. Just think of the experts we become as they get older!

Below are tips to provide effective limit setting with a positive approach:

Be Specific:

Stay clear and concise when requesting children to carry out a task or follow a rule. Example: If the rule is that they need to clean up one activity before they begin a new one, then we can say, "You can play with the Play-Doh after you clean up the blocks."

Give Some Choices:

Especially when our kids are at the age of exhibiting power struggles, giving them some choices can help.

However, giving them too may choices may be ineffective.

Example: When changing our two-year-old, we can ask, "Do you want to wear this shirt or that shirt?" Avoid too many options. Letting them decide between ten shirts may drive you and them crazy!

Be Firm, but Loving:

It's possible to have a firm tone and approach while extending a loving attitude. Example: If the blocks are still not picked up after asking once, in a firm voice, but not necessarily raising our voice, we can say, "Please pick up your blocks. After they are cleaned up, then you can play with the Play-Doh." Also, we need to keep in mind the importance of following through, and to not let our kids play with the Play-Doh if they don't pick up the blocks.

Utilize a Positive Approach:

There are a handful of positive approaches to consider when enforcing our limit setting. The choice of words we use and rephrasing words with a positive spin can make a difference. For example, referring to the Play-Doh scenario in the "Be Specific" section, "You can play with the Play-Doh after you clean up the blocks" is a positive approach versus saying, "You can't play with the Play-Doh until you clean up the blocks." Another positive approach is utilizing a fun and creative way to accomplish a task with our child. When it's time to get our two-year-old into the bedroom to change her pajamas, we can say with an upbeat voice and attitude, "Let's go change into your pajamas; I'm going to quack like a duck all the way to your room. What animal are you going to be?" There's a good chance our two-year-old will follow us after we start heading in that direction in a silly and "quacking" manner. Children *love* these games.

Follow Through with Consequences:

It is preferable to utilize a positive approach; however, after trying this angle, it may be clear that our child may just simply want to refuse whatever we are asking him to do. And we know how much fun it is when we reach this point! If it's a two-year-old refusing to go to his room to change his clothes, we can say, "If you are not in your room by the count of three, then I will help you into your room, and you will not have playtime before bed." If he continues to refuse, then assist or pick him up and place him into his room to be changed, without having playtime before bed. But let's not forget to give a loving hug to our child before he goes to sleep—apply "Be Firm, but Loving."

An example of following through with a consequence for an older child is, "It's dinnertime. I told you that if I had to ask you again to turn off the PlayStation, then you could not play with it for the rest of the evening. I'm going to turn it off now, and you have lost privileges with playing with your PlayStation for the rest of night." When the rules are established and our kids know the consequences, they have the opportunity to control their own outcome. It offers children lessons to learn by taking responsibility for choices they make.

Focus on Behavior—Not the Child:

If a child is exhibiting negative behavior, it's important to focus on the behavior, not labeling the child as "being bad." For example, if a three-year-old hits another child, we want to emphasize that the behavior is unacceptable, but avoid labeling the child. We can say, "We do not hit other people; we need to use our words." Then try to communicate the importance of this through further dialogue.

Make an Effort to Communicate:

The benefits of using an authoritative parenting style is that it encourages being firm, yet it emphasizes the importance of responsiveness and communicating with our children. When we are firm, it is also highly beneficial to discuss with our children the importance of the rule we are enforcing with age-appropriate words. It shows respect to our children and gives them the opportunity to learn from the experience.

Organizing Tips for Setting Limits

- Make a list of rules and post it for your children (if necessary, include pictures if your kids cannot yet read).
- When conveying the rules, keep your words positive such as, "We sit in our chairs; the food stays on our plate, not the floor; we take our shoes off before sitting on the couch."

LIFE LESSON #5

Promote Conflict Resolution Skills

Too often we give children answers to
remember rather than problems to solve.

Roger Lewin

Why Puppies and Babies Go So Well Together

Picture a supersoft, energetic puppy romping alongside a giggling, sweet-smelling baby crawling—both wobbling as they try to move about. Both little creatures bring us such joy, nurturing, and comfort—and both have little accidents: puppies unknowingly soil the newly installed carpet while babies do likewise in their freshly changed diapers. These innocent little ones are clearly dependent on others for food, care, and the learning of appropriate social behavior.

The more I thought about these similarities, it dawned on me that perhaps there is a teaching mechanism that works for my nontalking pup as well as my preverbal babe. While a bit embarrassing to admit, I came up with a learning strategy for my twins that grew out of my experience of, and love and tenderness for, my own puppy.

Instinctively, I have always had talent with puppies and dogs, which actually led to my hosting the first TV dog game show on Animal Planet called *Zig and Zag*. The game was based on agility and gave the dog handler and puppy the opportunity to share a bond beyond words. I've always felt that, developmentally, puppies land at the human age equivalency of two and a half years old. Puppies are naturally smart, alert, and willing to learn; however, they'll never talk. Kids, on the other hand, will have the advantage of actually "talking" as they age and will be verbally able to express their thoughts and feelings. Puppies communicate with their eyes, body language, and by making noises—much like my twins Ryker and Makenna did as babies. Since dogs can't formally understand English, or for that matter French, Spanish, or Chinese, it's imperative to be able to communicate with something other than words.

When I speak the word "sit" and the puppy sits, most people assume the puppy understands the word "sit." I could have said "teddy bear" and still trained my puppy to sit every time I said that word. The secret is the tone of my voice, my intention, and my consistency.

Being a forty-something mom and a busy professional TV host, I had to create a way for my twin toddlers to deal with the concept of sharing. My kids' concept of sharing at that time was screaming the word "MINE"—and it just wasn't working. Creatively and cautiously, I decided to try a Pavlov-inspired approach to the principles of sharing. I simply call it, "Count to Ten, My Turn." It's based on the reward principle of teaching, acknowledging good behavior, and consistency in effective nonverbal communication. Now I must preface all of this with the statement that I am not a doctor or psychologist, just a mother of twins and someone who has been able to teach her lovely, face-licking, cuddle-seeking puppy to respond to her requests.

Here is an example: When your young child has a toy and you ask him or her for it, inevitably they will say "no" or "mine" or just grab on to it tightly. Now, what I do is count to ten out loud, say "my turn" and take the toy. It's easy with twins because once you've counted to ten, you immediately give it to the other child. Implementing this technique, my friends who had an only child proved that it works just as well when you take the toy for yourself. This "sharing method" is especially useful when your second or third baby comes along. Start young, even before your child learns to speak, as you can simply count aloud for them.

I found as I frequently and consistently practiced this technique with my little ones, scientifically I had created a conditioned reflex. As my twins inevitably wanted to play with the same toy, I simply had them count to ten out loud and say "my turn"—it was magical! Pavlov may have discovered it worked for puppies, but I discovered peace and quiet in the Riley household, because we never "yelped" over toys.

Perfect example: We were visiting some friends on our street and the twins were playing with their three-year-old daughter. The other toddler had a toy that our Makenna wanted to play with, and she simply refused to share and started screaming, "IT'S MINE!" As her mother tried to discipline the little girl by offering her other toys and talking to her about the benefits of sharing (while she wailed and gripped the toy even tighter), we awkwardly dismissed ourselves for the evening. As we walked home my husband, Tom, pulled out a flashlight. Immediately, Ryker said, "Can I hold it?" Naturally, Makenna wanted to hold it as well. So they simply started counting, "1, 2, 3 . . . 10, my turn" back and forth, back and forth. My children must have shared that flashlight over thirty times as they walked down the street. Tom and I strolled hand in hand, enjoying the fresh evening air to the sound of "1, 2, 3, 4, 5, 6, 7, 8, 9, 10 . . . my turn."

Is it possible that my sweet little playful puppy could actually teach me something as important as resolving conflict between two toddlers? Yes, indeed! In fact, Pavlov would have reveled in the success of my creative idea, and I can't express how proud I was to watch my parenting philosophy in action—no fighting or screaming, just counting and sharing.

Forbes Riley

LIFE LESSON #5:

Utilizing effective communication and conflict resolution skills can be looked at as a philosophy—a commitment and a way of life. It is how we interact with our loved ones, acquaintances, and even perfect strangers that can make our world a better place. Integrating this idea into our parenting philosophy can fulfill the ethics and moral teachings that many of us busy moms strive to teach our children each and every day. It starts with us! Aside from children learning how to communicate and problem solve directly from their parents, the powerful effect on their learning process from observing how we interact with others is tremendous. Next time we have a disagreement with our spouse, a family member, or the person who just cut us off while driving, remember that our children are in fact processing and learning from our choices on how to use our conflict and resolution skills.

The first step is to examine how we view conflict and how effective we are with resolving differences. It might be helpful to ask ourselves, "How do I feel about experiencing conflicts? How effectively do I resolve conflicts with my significant other, family members, friends, and even strangers?"

The reality is, conflict is healthy, normal, and expected each and every day of our lives and at times can be very positive. It is how we choose to deal with conflict that really matters. We all have different perspectives and life experiences that result in seeing life through our own set of eyes.

A conflict is an expressed struggle between individuals or groups. It can be real or perceived. A conflict may also occur when one person perceives a problem and the other person or group doesn't realize there is an issue.

To effectively work through conflict, it is important to recognize that we all have basic human needs. They can be as basic as: **power, belonging, freedom, fun,** and **security.** In addition to identifying our own basic needs, it is imperative to think about others' basic needs in order to work through these struggles. For example, out of the five basic needs above, let's think about who would gravitate toward them. Most likely an infant's basic need would be **security** as they are completely dependent on their care-givers. A two-year-old typically has a great need for **power** (in the midst of their power struggles) and wanting to experience **fun**. Teenagers usually want **power, freedom, fun,** and a strong sense of **belonging**. Security tends to be the last thing on their minds. No wonder we worry about them so much! An older adult who just retired tends to have needs, such as **security** and **belonging**. The point of thinking through these basic needs is that when we are experiencing conflict with someone else, it's important to be sensitive to the needs they may be experiencing, so that we can better understand the whole situation.

When our two-year-olds are in the midst of a tantrum, although it can drive us crazy to the point of wanting to pull our hair out, let's remind ourselves that they are entering a developmental stage and need to work out their power struggles.

When our teenagers are slamming doors and angry because their curfew is earlier than the rest of their friends, let's remember that the only thing they tend to care about during this time in their lives is their need for **freedom, fun,** and to have that sense of **belonging** among their peer groups. Although we need to do our jobs as parents and reinforce the rules, it can make a difference when we are sensitive and acknowledge their frustrations, while we make an effort to talk it through with them.

When we, as busy moms, commit to improving our conflict resolution skills and integrate this idea into our parenting philosophy, it will not only manage our days more effectively, but it can also bring about a much greater quality of life.

Assumptions of Conflict

Assumption: There is nothing positive about conflict.

- In reality, conflict is inevitably a part of our everyday lives, and at times can be very positive.

Assumption: Conflict should be polite and orderly.

- In reality, conflict is often disorderly and confusing, which adds to authenticity.

Assumption: Anger is the predominant emotion in conflict interaction.

- In reality, there are many emotions involved (anger is just the tip of the iceberg).

Tips to Deal with Anger and Conflict Resolution

Anger often overshadows real and underlying feelings. For example, underlying feelings may consist of fear, rejection, or inadequacy. When anger is high, reasoning and judgment are low. It is difficult to work things out effectively when we are angry.

Tips to Deal with Anger

- Get to know your triggers; for example, when others roll their eyes at you.
- Get to know your physical symptoms or signals of anger; for example, face feeling hot.
- Identify techniques to calm yourself; for example (1) use a calm voice; (2) focus on listening to the other person; (3) deep breathing; (4) self-talk; (5) remove yourself from the situation if necessary to calm yourself; and (6) give up the need to "be right" and instead look for the solution.

Tips to Use Effective Conflict Resolution

- Remember that anger tends to come from fear. What are the parties fearful of? How does the fear trigger their anger?
- Avoid defensive and provoking statements.
- Avoid making judgments.
- Do not say, "You shouldn't be angry." Feelings are very real. Everyone has their own experience and perceptions in any given situation.
- Ask for suggestions on solving the problem together. Initiate collaborative suggestions yourself.
- Use productive negotiation techniques when the other person calms down. Until then, acknowledge feelings more than ideas.
- Recognize the importance that others are entitled to feel sadness and disappointment. We need to allow others to go through this process.

We extend a special appreciation to Dr. Susan Rice, Professor Emerita at California State University, Long Beach. A significant amount of this Life Lesson is from her course material on conflict resolution.

Essential Ingredient #3

IMPLEMENT CREATIVE SOLUTIONS (WITH AN ORGANIZED APPROACH)

We are what we repeatedly do.
Excellence then, is not an act, but a habit.

Aristotle

"If you have kids, this is the model for you."

LIFE LESSON #1

Have Essentials Ready to Go

Motherhood has a very humanizing effect.
Eveything gets reduced to essentials.

Meryl Streep

❧ Early-Morning Rush
....

Seven AM—the time of day every mother dreads. I remember, just a short time ago, how much I hated the morning rush. Every night I would clean up and prepare myself for the day that lay ahead. I was always so proud of myself—until I woke up in the morning. Suddenly, the baby needed to be nursed, the three-year-old had to be coerced into getting out of bed, while my older daughters fought over who got to use the bathroom first. There was inevitably a crisis because my eleven-year-old, who needed to wear her good luck white undershirt every day, couldn't find it. All this before we even sat down for breakfast!

No matter how hard I tried, or how much I prepared, I didn't know how to completely avoid the morning havoc that comes hand in hand with having a large family. It doesn't really matter if you have two children or ten; the morning is a constant struggle. With seven kids under the age of fourteen, I needed a way to involve all my children in helping me get out of the house in the morning in a timely manner. I had had enough of being late for school lineups and sweating and panting as if I had just run a marathon after I finally dropped the kids off in the morning.

Something had to be done. Luckily, the school my children attended required uniforms, so I wasn't subjected to the tormenting task of picking out outfits each day. Making sure each child had a clean shirt and run-free tights, however, was a different story. I began to organize each child's closet in the following manner. Each girl (there were six of them!) was given five hangers (for each day of the school week) that had skirt hanger attachments. In addition, each set of hangers was in a different color (pink, red, blue, purple, yellow, and green) that corresponded to the color of the thread that I had sewn into each daughter's undershirts, shirts, skirts, tights, and even underwear. I attached a heavy-duty ziplock bag to each hanger and put a fresh pair of underwear, tights and an undershirt in it each day. On the hanger went the shirt and skirt. All shoes lay at the front door, on a handy shoe rack. When the laundry was done, it was hung straight back on my handy outfit organizers.

Next I tackled the school lunches. I always found that we spent 50 percent more when we shopped hungry, so I started going to the market with my daughters after we ate a filling dinner. We all sat down and made a list first so that we knew what we were shopping for, and so we wouldn't waste time. I typed up this list, and every week I would review it with my daughters so they could add what they wanted. After our shopping adventure, we would all spend twenty minutes unpacking the food, immediately portioning it into baggies. These baggies would go straight into clear plastic boxes in the fridge and pantry, so that packing the lunches in the morning would be essentially painless. Having my children be a part of the food planning, shopping, and packing lightened my load immensely. Preparing lunches now took less time and was a group effort. Everyone was happy.

Finally, I created a backpack system to create order where there once had been chaos. Instead of the backpacks being flung haphazardly on the floor in the kitchen or the child's bedroom, they were placed on hooks in age order in the kitchen. I was able to go through the backpacks one by one to check for papers I had to sign, or homework I had to review. I also made sure that each child had a different colored/shaped backpack so that there would be no confusion. It was the girls' responsibility to make sure that their backpack was returned to the kitchen (if they had taken it upstairs to do homework) before they went to sleep. This way, I could tell with just a glance if the backpack was ready for a speedy departure in the morning.

To ensure total participation from the children, I began a bean jar reward system. I collected five jars of similar size and bought a package of kidney beans. For each good action, such as making her bed, brushing her teeth, and getting into the car on time, each child would get a bean. When the jar was full they could cash their beans in for money or a prize at the local discount store. For the girls, the beans represented something more real to them than any star chart system I had used. They delighted in seeing their jars fill up and counting the beans.

Needless to say, my morning rush to school became significantly less . . . rushed. I never did figure out a way to get out of nursing the baby at breakfast or how to make the phone stop ringing. (Why does anyone call at 8:00 AM anyway?) But I did learn how to make the most of my morning and how to plan ahead. I always wondered, though, if my kids realized how much these tactics were helping them, or if they just thought I was crazy with all my planning.

My kids have grown up a lot by now, and I really only have to get the youngest two ready for school. My oldest is married and has her own child. The other day she called me with excitement in her voice.

"Mom," she said. "Today I folded Ari's clothes just like you taught me to, and I organized them into outfits for each day of the week! Aren't you proud of me?" I was proud of her, but also, my heart warmed at the realization that after all these years, my daughter was proud of me too.

Esther Simon

LIFE LESSON #1:

How many of us can relate to the following scenarios:

We're out and about and our five-month-old has an "explosion," and it is making its way out of the diaper!

In the midst of a stroll, our one-year-old throws his pacifier down in the gutter with grungy water flowing.

We're out doing errands with our toddler and it is taking much longer than we anticipated. Our toddler is hungry AND we have no snacks in sight!

Our three-year-old realizes she can't hold it in and says that she needs to make a "poopy"—oh, and by the way, there is no bathroom in sight!

Our ten-year-old decides that he's going to slide into home base as if he's on a baseball field; however, he chooses to do this on the cement, and now there's a good-size gash on his knee!

We are driving our thirteen-year-old to school and just as we're pulling up, she says, "Oh no, I forgot my school report."

The following are organizing tips to help have "essentials" ready to go, and are broken up by age groups. Organizing can help decrease our stress and minimize the time we're running around last minute trying to get together the most basic items.

Infants/Toddlers

Keep the following in the diaper bag:

- diapers
- "poopy" bags
- baby wipes, antibacterial solution, and diaper cream
- a changing pad or disposable changing sheets
- extra sets of clothes (include socks)
- a sweater
- first aid items
- extra pacifiers, an extra bottle, and formula
- burp cloths, bibs, and tissues
- a few age-appropriate toys

For Infants and Toddlers: Keep in Mind the Climate You Live In—Freezing or 110°F Weather?

If you keep a diaper bag in the car, consider the weather. Keep baby wipes, antibacterial wipes, and diaper cream in the diaper bag or keep them in a small bag ready to go near the front door. And for toddlers, it's always a good idea to have nonperishable "backup" snacks in the car, as well as a bag in the house that's ready to go with some fresh snacks in it.

As a side note: another helpful hint—if you're not going to be too far from the car, keep a small bag with handles and put in some basic items you may need (for example, a book, Sippy Cup, snacks, tissues, antibacterial wipes, and one diaper with some baby wipes and a disposable changing sheet). We know how irritating it is to search throughout the whole diaper bag just to find the tissues, when instead we can grab a bag with some basic items in it.

Preschoolers

Keep the following in the car:

- diapers, baby wipes, "poopy" bags, changing disposable pads, and pacifiers (if still pertinent). Even if potty trained, keep extra sets of clothes and socks.
- antibacterial wipes and tissues
- toilet paper in case you need to "pretend you're camping" if your child needs to go potty outdoors
- a sweater
- first aid items
- age-appropriate toys
- "backup" snacks and water in the car, as well as a bag in the house that's ready to go with some fresh snacks in it

Also (as mentioned above in the infant section), when you're out and about with your children, consider taking a small bag with handles and putting in some basic items you may need, such as a pair of underwear and shorts, wipes and a "poopy" bag (just in case), some snacks, and a book.

School-Age

Keep the following in the car:

- a sweater
- an extra set of clothes (including socks)
- antibacterial wipes and tissues
- first aid items
- snacks and water
- activities that are "car friendly"
- extra batteries for the handheld games

Keep your school-age kids in the habit of having the following ready to go:

- food/snacks and a drink that they will want for later
- backpack for school ready to go (the night before)
- items that are needed for extracurricular activities (ready the night before)

In addition to storing first aid/emergency items in your car, it is always a great idea to keep a large towel in there as well. You never know when you're going to need it—whether it's for a picnic, the beach, or an unexpected mess!

Adults

We must not forget ourselves; we need our essentials too! How often do we forget the most basic items that we'll need throughout the day? We are so focused on making sure that we have everything together for our kids, that we sometimes forget to gather the essentials that keep us going throughout the day.

Keep the following in the car and/or purse:

- ibuprofen
- feminine products (especially if we're irregular!)
- tissues
- a few makeup items/pocket mirror (the simplicity of putting on some fresh lipstick can make a difference)
- bottled water
- paper products (little baggies, plates, paper towels, etc.—we never know when they'll come in handy)
- handy, healthy snacks
- a favorite magazine (for those brief and rare times when we're out and about and have a handful of minutes where we may actually have time to read)
- paperback for the long-waiting appointments
- mobile phone car charger
- spare change for parking meters
- pad and pen for thoughts, notes, and to-dos

LIFE LESSON #2

Have Creative Games/ Activities Ready to Go

The world of reality has limits; the world
of imagination is boundless.

Jean-Jacques Rousseau

✿ The Treasure Bag

In the early 1960s I was a Girl Scout aspiring to earn as many badges as possible. Since I leaned more toward the domestic side than the athletic side, this was more difficult than you would think. One of the badges I was after was the child care badge. To earn this, I solicited the moms in my Bergen County neighborhood, who were only too happy to have me take their young ones off their hands for a few hours a day at no cost to them.

I developed a "treasure bag" into which I placed puppets, storybooks, paper, crayons, balls, and cards with the names of games written on them with which I planned on entertaining my young charges. My backyard was our playground on sunny days, and our basement became an indoor playground when it rained. That summer was filled with games of "teacher," hide-and-seek, coloring contests, and puppet shows. I was the Pied Piper of Oak Ridge Road! And, I had more than enough hours to earn that coveted badge plus the first aid badge, since I had the opportunity to bandage a few bruises and heal make-believe fractures along the way.

Being a teenager who could never have enough money,

I once again went to the "treasure bag" and began babysitting for profit. The children looked forward to what I would bring in the bag for the evening's entertainment, and the parents trusted me because I had added the "question sheet for parents"—emergency numbers, where they would be, children's bedtimes—things that make a parent feel good. I was probably one of the most popular babysitters in my neighborhood because of that bag!

My first child, a daughter, was born in May 1990. I was obsessed with being the "perfect" mom. Everything we did was a learning experience for my daughter—I think she learned her letters from trips to the supermarket where I pointed out everything that was at eye level. However, our daily trips to the "Hippo Playground" at Riverside Park were my sanity savers—except when I was so frazzled getting out of the house that I forgot something important like diapers, juice, or wipes, or took so long getting myself together, we didn't get out of the house until late afternoon.

It was after one of those days that I sat on my sofa and reflected on how much simpler my life used to be. *Why couldn't I get out of the house early? Why was I forgetting things?* When I went to work every day, I was prepared—I had a briefcase. I thought back to how I had taken care of the neighbor's children and remembered my "treasure bag." Eureka! That's it! Plan ahead—be organized! That evening I found a canvas bag and stocked it with diapers, baby wipes, and juice boxes so I was ready to go the following day. As my daughter got older, I added bubbles, chalk, balls, finger foods, one and sometimes two changes of clothing, and Band-Aids. Each evening I restocked the bag.

I became one of the first parents to reach the playground daily. When my friends asked me about my transformation, I showed them my "treasure bag." I suddenly became the go-to mom when someone needed something.

As my daughter got older and a second daughter was born, multiple "treasure bags" lined my closet wall. (Hooks in closets are great for organizing your bags.) One was stocked with knee and elbow pads, wrist guards, and Band-Aids for skateboard/scootering outings; another held supplies to entertain the girls when we were traveling—games, music, paper and markers, and never to be forgotten AA batteries for an electronic game or a Walkman that were added at the last minute.

Now my children are older and don't rely on me to carry their necessities for them. But on those sunny summer mornings when we want to go to the beach, my indispensable "treasure bag" is in the hallway closet filled with clean towels, suntan lotion, sunglasses, and a good book—ready to go!

Karen Krugman

Life Lesson #2:

How often are we driving around with our antsy children in the backseat or we're trying to pass time while waiting for the meals to arrive at a restaurant? Engaging in activities to keep our children occupied when we're out and about can save the day. And, starting from the toddler stage, there are verbal activities that don't require us to bring a thing!

Worthwhile activities when you're on the go:
Infants
- "Safe" hand toys
- Books that are okay if they put them in their mouth
- Sing songs, even if you're making them up!
- Made-up songs that include colors, shapes, and body parts

Toddlers and Preschool Age
- Keep some crayons in your purse and scratch paper in the car. You never know when you could use them!
- Think about the numerous learning activities you can do while you're driving with your children or waiting for an appointment. Such as:
  - While driving: "It's a green light—we can go now. It's a red light—now we need to stop. Now I'm going straight; now I'm making a left turn . . ."

- Play books or songs on CDs for them to listen to and follow along.
- Talk about the colors you see while driving—the color of the cars and the color of leaves you see on the trees.
- Talk about the weather, the day of the week, and the current month.
- Talk about all the sizes and shapes around you. Whichever way you look, there is typically something that can be used as a learning experience with colors, numbers, shapes, letters, and various concepts.
- Play a game that entails thinking of an object and your kids need to guess what it is. You can give them clues, "It's blue and in the shape of a square . . ."
- Buy toys that are "mess free"—keep them in the car for availability as needed.

School-Age

- While driving, play fun games related to license plates from out of state.
- Ask your kids to keep some of their favorite magazines, books, crossword puzzles, and handheld computer games in the car to have available when they want them. As previously mentioned, have extra batteries on hand.

READER/CUSTOMER CARE SURVEY

HEMG

We care about your opinions! Please take a moment to fill out our online Reader Survey at **http://survey.hcibooks.com**. As a **"THANK YOU"** you will receive a **VALUABLE INSTANT COUPON** towards future book purchases as well as a **SPECIAL GIFT** available only online! Or, you may mail this card back to us.

First Name		MI.	Last Name

Address			City

State	Zip	Email	

1. Gender
❑ Female   ❑ Male

2. Age
❑ 8 or younger
❑ 9-12   ❑ 13-16
❑ 17-20   ❑ 21-30
❑ 31+

3. Did you receive this book as a gift?
❑ Yes   ❑ No

4. Annual Household Income
❑ under $25,000
❑ $25,000 - $34,999
❑ $35,000 - $49,999
❑ $50,000 - $74,999
❑ over $75,000

5. What are the ages of the children living in your house?
❑ 0 - 14   ❑ 15+

6. Marital Status
❑ Single
❑ Married
❑ Divorced
❑ Widowed

Comments

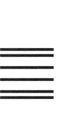

BUSINESS REPLY MAIL

FIRST-CLASS MAIL   PERMIT NO 45   DEERFIELD BEACH, FL

POSTAGE WILL BE PAID BY ADDRESSEE

Health Communications, Inc.
3201 SW 15th Street
Deerfield Beach FL 33442-9875

- Do communication-builder activities, such as asking your kids about their favorite book, music, or movie; why is it their favorite?
- A great game to play to pass time driving in the car is the "ABC" game. Before you arrive at the destination, look at street signs, signage on buildings, billboards, and license plates. Find items that begin with each letter and keep the letters in order. This can be played as a group or individually.

Also, when you have thirty minutes to spare before leaving the house, here are quick, worthwhile activities to fill that half-hour gap. In addition, these activities can even promote our little ones' prewriting skills. Part of the writing process is that young children need to strengthen their intrinsic muscles (the muscles that move the palm and the fingers) so they don't tire easily when writing. Engaging in hand manipulation activities gives them greater opportunity to achieve stronger writing skills.

Worthwhile activities to keep accessible at home:
- Just kneading Play-Doh in itself is a great activity.
- Push items such as coins or marbles into Play-Doh for your kids to find, if age appropriate.
- String dry cereal to make a cereal necklace/bracelet (pipe cleaners for little ones is easier).

- Place stickers on targets. For example, use colored markers and put small circles all over a piece of paper. Then, let your child put stickers on all the blue dots, followed by the green dots, followed by the yellow dots and so on.
- Finger painting is always a great activity—even with soap foam, shaving cream, or whip cream.
- Form letters and numbers with Play-Doh or pipe cleaners.

Below are additional easy and fun activities that can promote children's oral motor skills. This can help further their speech development and give them greater ability to enhance their skill-set to articulate words in conversational speech.

- Do cotton ball races (blowing a cotton ball with a straw).
- Blow paint from a straw: consider placing newspaper on the porch or backyard; place paint on paper and have your child blow out air through a straw so they can see the paint splatter. *Note: Make sure your child can blow the paint and won't try to suck it in!*
- Blow bubbles.

LIFE LESSON #3

Keep Age-Appropriate Items
in Each Key Room of the House

For every minute spent in organizing,
an hour is earned.

Unknown

✿ Ending Toy Room Cleanup Trauma

A friend once asked me if I used the cleanup song made popular by the TV character Barney to motivate my kids. "No," I replied, "the one I use goes something like this: 'If you don't get those toys cleaned up right this second I am going to throw them out!'"

Unfortunately the only thing my cleanup song accomplished was to vent my frustration. If I felt overwhelmed by the mess, then certainly my preschoolers didn't know where to start either. *How would they learn to take care of their belongings if I didn't teach them?* As the mother of three kids under five, I wasn't sure I could muster up the energy for an "extra" project. But I knew that if I didn't, our future would be filled with more of the same yelling, frustration, and lessons unlearned.

Two factors became obvious: we had too many toys and the toys weren't grouped in a way that made sense to the kids.

We needed toys placed in key areas where we spent the most time. Our main stomping grounds included the family room, kitchen, kid's bedrooms, and playroom. First,

I gathered toys from around the house and dumped them into one room. *If I crawl under this monstrosity, I mused, no one would find me for days.*

As good as that sounded, I knew my toy frustrations wouldn't just disappear. I got to work. Starting on one side of the pile, I sorted toys into categories. Baby toys went in one group, trucks in another, puzzles and games in another. The minipiles were designated by child or by type (for example, kitchen set toys). Once the items were grouped I could see how many duplicates we had. And so could my children.

At this point I asked my three-year-old son to choose which dump trucks he wanted to keep and which he could share with another little boy who didn't have any. My five-year-old daughter did the same with her dolls. Each child found items he or she no longer played with on a regular basis. Although it took longer to involve the kids in this step, it avoided later confrontations over where I put their toys. Even better, it taught them the value of being selective and the joy of sharing.

I placed a couple of toys in a rainy-day box, but gave the majority away. Whenever I felt the urge to reconsider, I remembered that having too many toys made it hard for them to find their favorites and impossible to put away. By creating a limit for how many stuffed animals they could have, they were gaining skills to know how much was enough.

After reducing the amount of toys, I designated where they would go. In our main play area, I created zones of like toys, similar to how their preschool arranges the room. We have a dress-up area, a place for the boy's toys, the girl's toys, the baby sister's toys, puzzles and games, and a craft area. I measured the available shelving and purchased inexpensive plastic containers to fit. Because covers are often hard for little hands to open, I just leave the covers off the bins.

Not everyone has the luxury of a separate playroom. The secret to maintaining a somewhat adult space in a family room while coexisting with children's toys is in container choice. Rather than buy one of those brightly colored kid's storage shelves that only match your decor if you live in a crayon box, purchase a bookcase and use attractive and sturdy baskets to slide onto the shelves. The shortest kid gets the lowest shelf. That way kids gain instant access to all their treasures and you won't have to look at playthings all over the floor. Bins naturally limit the amount of toys. When the baskets overflow, it's time to relocate toys or give some away. Don't forget to measure the shelves before you buy the baskets, and, for safety's sake, anchor the shelf to the wall with an L bracket or shelf brace.

Unless you love the feeling of a child clinging to your leg while you make dinner, consider creating play possibilities in your kitchen. I've made a lower cabinet child friendly with plastic containers, beat-up pans, bowls, and wooden spoons for instant musical entertainment. I've realized that the kitchen police will not arrest me if I keep toys, rather than just plates, in my kitchen cabinets. Another option is to create a portable arts center by repurposing a cleaning tote. The divided sections easily contain crayons, washable markers, stickers, paper, stencils, and anything else to occupy my young artists so I can chop in peace.

So far I had sorted, purged, measured, and bought containers. All that remained was to place the sorted toys into zones in my home's key areas and label the containers so everyone (including Dad) knew where to put them back. For example, the kitchen play set, play food, and doll crib went in one corner so when the kids play house they have everything they need right there. This also eliminates the step of wondering where something goes. The doll clothes go by the doll crib. The blocks go in the container labeled "blocks" next to the other building toys.

My three- and five-year-olds loved helping me label the containers. We taped on computer printed words plus a sticker or cutout from the box directly onto the clear container or on card stock attached to the basket with ribbon. Not only did the labels guide the kids in cleaning up toys, but it reinforced their pre-reading skills. Finally, we toured our new toy areas and discussed how we would work together to tidy up.

I am happy to report that I no longer wave around a garbage bag threatening to trash their mess. Instead we spend five to ten minutes before bed putting away toys in each of our main play areas. Not only is our house calmer, but I feel like I am equipping them with skills they need as adults: to keep the things they love, to give to others, and to take care of their belongings. In the end, it's not about the stuff; it's about building good habits that last a lifetime.

Kate Varness

✿

LIFE LESSON #3:

Depending on the developmental age of children, some need more supervising than others, and some need more entertaining than others. And for those children who need a lot of our attention, we want to balance this with helping them find creative ways to self-entertain. Also, when caring for more than one child, especially when they're quite young and need constant supervision, there is an art to caring for all of our children simultaneously. When we as busy moms think ahead and prepare for this scenario, and when age-appropriate items are in each key room of the house, it can truly help transform our busy days.

For those of us with infants, keeping a stroller in the house can save the day when our precious little ones are in that stage of screaming every time we stop holding them. It's useful, especially for us moms who are prone to our backs giving out from wearing a baby sling. Rocking our infants next to us in a stroller while we're preparing a meal gives them the opportunity to see us as we can take one foot and move the stroller back and forth and engage with them. The stroller can also allow us to eat and use the bathroom while our baby engages with us simultaneously. There's nothing worse than heading toward the bathroom and hearing our baby in the background screaming her head off! Now, for the busy moms who have older kids and are past the infancy stage, doesn't life seem just a tad easier? Okay, maybe just different, but well worth it with all the amazing love and experiences that we do have with our little ones as they grow up!

Also, with infants, we know how important "tummy time" is and giving them the chance to just hang out on the floor. Think through the key places where we spend time in the house and place a nice thick blanket, burp cloths, and some basic baby toys in a basket. Perhaps in our bedroom, the living room area, and an older child's bedroom?

When we are in the midst of caring for our older and younger children, keeping age-appropriate items in the key rooms of the house can be very helpful as we're busily trying to take care of all matters. For example, if we're hanging out in our eight-year-old's room helping hang up her clothes—and we're trying to entertain our nine-month-old simultaneously—it can make a big difference to keep a basket of age-appropriate toys that we're able to pull out of our eight-year-old's closet.

When children are bored or do not have age-appropriate items in which to engage, it can turn into—well, let's just say—an ugly situation! Sometimes it's the small organizational ideas that can make the bigger difference when we achieve all of our tasks as busy moms. By planning in advance, we are also able to accomplish another important goal: creating time with our kids, making it as enjoyable as possible and filled with positive experiences.

Organizing Tips

- Decide which rooms in the house are key rooms (where you spend the most time).
- Select baskets or bags to hold basic items and toys that you can pull out the moment you need it.
- Make a point of replenishing these baskets/bags at the beginning of each month.
- Have a box of tissues and a container of antibacterial solution readily available in key spots throughout the house. This enables you to keep the germs away as you wipe your little ones' noses. Older kids can help

themselves to disinfecting their hands after blowing their noses. It's always ideal to wash hands, but the antibacterial solution can make a difference in the absence of hand washing to avoid colds. We all know how when someone gets sick in the home, it's a matter of days before the whole household is sick!

LIFE LESSON #4

Involve Your Kids with Cleaning/Chores

*Now, as always, the most automated
appliance in a household is the mother.*

Beverly Jones

৵❀ Missy's Menagerie

Old and new homework papers spilling out of back-packs, floor covered with heaps of questionably clean clothes, the bed populated with a menagerie of stuffed animals—my new client was a thirteen-year-old with a bedroom that needed organization.

"Missy" was giving me a tour of the clutter zones, and as she tugged on the closet door, it popped open, releasing an avalanche of more than 400 stuffed animals.

Missy and her mom had reached an impasse over the fate of the animals. I was there as a neutral third party to help evaluate, de-clutter, and organize the room to reflect her new teenage status. Additionally, Mom wanted her daughter to learn how to make choices and "let go of stuff" in a positive and mindful way.

A motivated thirteen-year-old is a joy to work with, and Missy began sorting with enthusiasm. We set up a string of large boxes: donation, garage sale, keep, maybes, and most important, precious treasures.

Clothes were first on the agenda, and she quickly filled the boxes with outgrown or "roadkill" (translation—yucky) items. Deeply buried, the first treasure soon emerged, a long-lost CD case filled with favorite songs. Missy was ecstatic and said that finding it made the whole day a success.

Finally the closet was accessible, and Missy plunked down on the floor while I began heaving out a stream of Beanie Babies, bears, frogs, and giant chair critters that almost buried her.

As she sorted, Missy shared with me that when her parents were divorcing three years ago, she was sad and depressed. She knew that after the divorce was finalized, they would be moving out of their home. Her dad would leave town, and she would be changing schools and moving away from her friends. To soothe some of the loss, Missy and her mother would go almost every day to buy another stuffed animal. The animals became her dearest friends, and she would tell them all her fears and sorrows. We talked about how important the animals were to her during that difficult transition, and Missy decided she wanted to honor them. I suggested we take photographs of her surrounded by all the animals she was giving away so she would always remember them. As I snapped pictures, Missy chatted away to each animal, thanking it for being such a special friend and explaining to it that some other kid would love it as much as she did. Then she would kiss and hug it and happily throw it into the appropriate box.

Missy was refreshingly verbal, connected to her feelings

and comfortable with me. At first she struggled to decide between favorites "Fluffy" the bunny and "Dino" the dinosaur. She loved to cuddle and hug "Big Bear" and "Lillie the Kitty." I asked her to think about her animals in categories of "friends," "acquaintances," or "strangers," and decisions suddenly became easier. Animals she didn't even recall buying—strangers—went away quickly. Friends, Missy's well-loved buddies, were set aside to populate the room in places of honor. Now she only had acquaintances to choose between, with criteria such as "are you huggable or stiff," "cute or ugly," or "have I grown away from you?" to determine their fate.

Mom was sensitive to her commitment to stay out of our way and appeared only to remove bulging garbage bags, garage sale and donation boxes, and to applaud Missy's progress. She also answered the doorbell, rung impatiently by Missy's friends who wanted to play with her.

Now the population of Missy's menagerie was cut in half, to less than 200 toys, and her creative juices started to flow as she saw her bedroom's potential. Towers of colorful "cubbies" went into the closet for easy access to stack her jeans, Ts, shorts, and tops. We identified laundry as an organizing pitfall and adopted the theory that as long as clothes transitioned smoothly from dryer to drawer, cubbie or basket, that "unfolded is OK." Socks went into the top dresser drawer, undies in the next. Missy's confidence grew as her creative personality infused the room.

A follow-up call two weeks later brought me up-to-date. Our momentum had inspired Missy to initiate a de-cluttering in the guest room. "Mom, it's nothing but a dumping ground!" They powered through it in one morning, generating more garage sale items. And that threatened garage sale actually happened.

Missy said at first she felt sad seeing her toys leave, but then she saw how excited the kids who bought them were. Counting up the proceeds from the sale sent her spirits soaring when the grand total reached almost $100—a healthy boost toward their upcoming Hawaiian vacation fund.

Missy reported that her room is easy to keep picked up, and the closet system worked well. Now that the floor is visible, she and her new girlfriends hang out in the room, and she frequently has sleepovers. What a difference from a year ago when Missy was the odd-one-out socially and having a tough time adjusting to her new school.

Missy's menagerie had supported her emotionally during the difficult changes in her family and her transition into junior high, but with her thirteenth birthday, she had reached a tipping point. It was time to make some changes. With just a little support and encouragement, her room project became a pivotal opportunity for her to learn about taking ownership of her possessions, become actively involved in the household, and make her own choices and decisions as she enters her teen years.

Heidi N. Schulz

ॐ

LIFE LESSON #4:

Completing chores, such as doing laundry, cleaning the house, taking out the trash, washing dishes, and sorting through the mail were tasks we managed during the days prior to children. Even then, it seemed like there was never enough time to keep up. Achieving these chores now as busy moms with a toddler holding on to our leg as we're trying to throw out the trash, or folding laundry as our two-year-old is trying to help, certainly slows down the process even more. And for those of us who have teenagers, it's as if they don't know a trash can or a laundry bin even exists!

Then, the thought of going to the market, the post office, or on other errands that require more than ten minutes of our time can create more of a challenge than the best of us moms ever knew existed. This is especially challenging with young children and for those of us who refer to our little ones as "strong-willed" children.

The following are organizing tips for busy moms to accomplish tasks and to creatively include our kids in the process.

Ideas for Infants

Although we know the importance and cherish the bonding experience when we engage with our babies by cooing with them or singing to them, we also know the need to complete certain tasks during our very busy days. And, typically at the end of the day, when we haven't had one minute to slow down, it feels like we didn't get the chance to get anything done!

There are some infants that are completely content with "tummy time" on the floor mat with cool hanging items in front of them to bat. They may also spend time in their bouncy seat with more neat things to grab and manipulate, or enjoy the baby swing with music in the background.

Then there are infants who scream their heads off the moment we put them down. Although we have tremendous love for our babies, and there are numerous amazing moments throughout our days with our little ones, let's face it—it can also be utterly exhausting! Naturally there is the baby sling, which can be an amazing experience for both mom and baby. We as moms tend to feel very connected and bonded with our babies as they are lying next to our beating heart. Our babies stay connected to us as they experience movements as if they were still in our womb. However, after a period of time, our backs and shoulders can begin to ache. So, this brings us back to the idea of utilizing a stroller in the house. Many infants crave the motion, and it allows our babies to stay with us as we engage in our daily tasks.

Ideas for Toddlers/Preschoolers

Typically, our toddlers and preschoolers want more than ever to just hang out with us, as they desire our attention and affection. They usually want to do "grown-up things." Finding ways for kids to participate in tasks and chores that we would rather not do happens to be something that they tend to get excited about.

Tips while cleaning the house:

- Give your child a wet paper towel and let him wipe the chairs or any other surfaces and aspects of the house that are okay.
- Purchase a miniature-size broom and dustpan to let your child participate in sweeping.
- Give them a small bag of garbage to throw out (with not too much trash) when you go out to the trash bin.
- Try to make it fun by singing songs together or period-ically just acting plain old silly.
- Consider letting your older preschooler help vacuum with the DustBuster.

Tips while doing laundry:

- After you sort the clothes for the wash, your kids can help put the clothes in the washer. Let them add soap and push the "start" button. They can also help when the clothes are ready for the dryer.

- When folding the clothes, give your child a small pile to fold. This is also a great learning activity for sorting, learning colors, counting, and recognizing patterns. Prior to folding the clothes, we can say, "Let's put the blue-colored clothes in this pile and the white colors here. Now let's count how many pieces of blue clothes we have . . ."

Tips while going through the mail:

- "Junk mail" often seems ten times thicker than important mail. Give the junk mail to your kids for them to open as you sift through your own. This way they are "helping" you sort through the mail.
- During the holidays, let your children take turns opening the holiday cards.

Tips while going to the market:

- Kids love to participate in finding the needed food items and putting them in the cart. Also, when going through the produce aisles, it's a great opportunity for them to learn their fruits, veggies, and colors. They can then help count out how many will go into the bag.
- When your kids are in the stroller, talk to them

throughout the process of marketing and have them hold certain items as you're strolling along.

- Your toddler might be in a stage where it seems just impossible to take her to the market or on similar errands. This is when you truly need to summon all your creative energies and think of different alternatives. Consider doing whatever possible to see if someone else can watch your child while completing your errands. Of course, kids go through phases, and hopefully this phase will pass sooner than later!

- Consider letting your child use a kid's shopping cart for markets that provide one.

- Teach your older kids price comparisons so they can learn the value of money; also show children nutritional labels to understand how they can eat healthier.

Ideas for School-Age Kids/Teenagers

When we engage our school-age kids and our teenagers with cleaning and chores, we are helping them prepare for the years to come. So much of our daily routine and how we operate comes from our habits. If we engage our kids in worthwhile habits while they're growing up, there's a better chance that it will stick with them when they hit the real world. When we teach our kids to keep a clean home environment, this can also help them stay organized, which is a tremendous contributing factor toward achieving success.

Tips to help kids with cleaning and chores:

- Keep a list posted with each of your kids' chores and rotate the chores if you have more than one child.
- Remind your kids that they'll get to enjoy their activity of (fill in the blank) after they complete their tasks.
- Consider giving your kids something special at the end of the week if they've done a great job with their chores. Although we don't want our children to solely rely on incentives when completing tasks, depending on the circumstances, it's possible it can make a significant difference. Adults experience various incentives, such as a paycheck at the end of the day (of course that's if we work outside of the home). There are occasions when kids may also need certain enticements.

Note: Please refer to Essential Ingredient #5, Life Lesson #4 for to-do lists that your school-age or teenager can utilize.

LIFE LESSON #5

Have a "Creative Center" Available

I see the mind of the five-year-old
as a volcano with two vents:
destructiveness and creativeness.

Sylvia Ashton Warner

The Art of Connection: My Daughter and Myself

I am the mother of a nine-year-old daughter and twelve-year-old son. Last night after homework, dinner, and a day full of multitasking, I sank into my desk chair at the computer to complete the very last entry on my to-do list—answer business and personal e-mails. My nine-year-old daughter, Sedona, came into my office carrying a sketch pad and a pencil. She pulled up a stool and asked, "Can I draw you, Mommy, as you work at the computer?" "Sure," I agreed, secretly relieved that she was giving me permission to continue responding to an e-mail from a client who was seeking advice. My fingers clicked away at the keys with suggestions. Suddenly, I stopped. In this moment, I had a choice: play with words in cyberspace about parenting or be a parent and share a warm moment of intimacy with my daughter. I had recently heard the expression that "as a parent the days are long, but the years are short." I pulled my fingers away from the keyboard and smiled at her—giving her my full attention.

As I watched her, I felt a rush of delight that she was drawing with the art supplies that we had bought together recently. I love doing artwork and collecting different art supplies; I wanted to share that with my daughter. I had taken her to a supply store full of new treasures: perfectly sharpened pencils, crisp white pads of paper, brilliant wands of colors and brushes. We had brought a selection home and Sedona had organized them into little baskets on a tray in the center of a small table in her room. Now she was using them. I sat still as she drew me. I wondered who she was seeing and what I looked like as her mother. After a few minutes, she held up the picture: a contour drawing of my face and body. I expressed my appreciation and was quietly impressed with her attention to detail.

I then asked if she wanted me to draw her. Her face lit up. She eagerly handed me the pencil and pad. I started to feel pangs of doubt about my ability—I hadn't sketched in a while. I secretly worried that I might be unable to draw her as she might like to be seen. As I gazed at my daughter, my hands easily sketched the curves and shadows of her face. It was as if the cells in my body seemed to remember how my womb had participated in helping her body form, just as the form was now being created on the paper. She seemed to enjoy my eyes studying her features and expression. Silently watching her reminded me of the many hours that I spent looking into her eyes when I breast-fed her. As I drew her, I felt a rush of love, calm, and caring. I showed her the drawing. "I like how you drew me, Mommy!" she said. As if I had just received a good grade in school, I was so happy that she liked the sketch. We both looked at the masterpieces; they would be a reminder of our very focused time. She grasped both pictures and ran downstairs to put them up on the refrigerator, just as I had done with much of the preschool artwork that she had created.

Now when I see the drawings, I smile and remember the calm, serene moment that my daughter and I shared together—how the transformation of a pad of paper by a pencil and loving hands can nourish the souls of the artist and the admirers. I must remember to keep that tray of art supplies filled when she is a teenager so that we can continue on with the art of connection.

Lauren Martin Culp

LIFE LESSON #5:

It's a good idea to consider keeping a "creative center" in our homes with age-appropriate supplies just for the kids. While we as busy moms are trying to take care of chores in the house, this creative center can provide a wonderful outlet for our kids to tap into their creative minds and enhance their self-expression. This is also a fantastic avenue for the kids who tend to shy away from verbally communicating their feelings. When we keep it organized, functional, and with easy access, our kids can get the items they need themselves and then put the items back when they're finished. For toddlers, preschool, and school-age children, it may be helpful to set up the center in the kitchen so that if it gets a bit messy, it's easier to clean up.

For Toddlers/Preschool Ages:

- Use age-appropriate table and chairs.
- Provide easy-access drawer and/or bin space for items next to and on the table.
- Consider stocking this area with the following items, but be sure that the easily accessible ones are developmentally and age-appropriate for your children. For example, some toddlers are prone to eating the Play-Doh, while others are not.

  - Play-Doh & accessories
  - crayons
  - markers
  - child safety scissors
  - glue
  - items for painting
  - stickers
  - plain paper
  - construction paper
  - chalk and chalkboard
  - arts & crafts items (e.g., feathers, yarn, buttons, etc.)

Also, if we have a wall near the creative center, children love seeing their artwork displayed. However, we may want to have a rule that only a certain amount of items can be hung. And every time they want to hang a new picture, they must decide which one to take down.

For School-Age Children:

- Their own small table with chairs.
- Easy-access drawer and bin space.
- Consider stocking this area with the following:
  - ◆ colored pencils, crayons, markers, chalk and chalkboard
  - ◆ scissors, glue, arts and crafts items, paper, stickers
  - ◆ different mediums of painting (water, paint-by-numbers, etc.)
  - ◆ beads for kids to make bracelets and necklaces
  - ◆ model-making items (such as a model plane kit)

For Teenagers:

- Consider an "art table" or a desk.
- Provide a drawer and/or bin space.
- In addition to all the items in the "school-age" category, consider oil paints, scrapbook materials, and modeling clay.

Beware! We may find ourselves wanting to engage in the creative center just as much as the kids. We tend to focus on numerous task-oriented agendas throughout our days in order to keep the household functioning, and we neglect our creative side. Although we often encounter difficulty finding "alone time" to nurture this aspect of ourselves, at least we can tap into creative juices with our kids! And without even realizing it, this creative center can also lend itself to random conversations with our kids, which can enhance the parent-child relationship.

"My Mom's busy. I'm taking her calls!"

Essential Ingredient #4

FEED YOUR SOUL

If a man does not keep pace with his
companions, perhaps it is because he hears
a different drummer. Let him step
to the music he hears, however
measured or far away.

Henry David Thoreau

LIFE LESSON #1

Redefine Your Identity

Knowing others is wisdom.
Knowing oneself is enlightenment.

Lao Tzu

❧ You know you're a mom when . . .

1. You plan your day according to when *Sesame Street* is on.
2. You have signed a check with a crayon.
3. You find Goldfish crackers in the glove box of your car.
4. You wipe other kids' noses.
5. You have accidentally brushed your teeth with Desitin.
6. You have caught spit-up in your hand.
7. You leave for a date with your husband carrying a diaper bag instead of your purse.
8. You have memorized the entire lineup of Saturday morning cartoons.
9. You have finally paid for all of your groceries and are heading out of the doors when you realize one of your kids has lost a shoe somewhere in the store.
10. You can recite *Goodnight Moon* and *Green Eggs and Ham* by heart.
11. You let your baby sit in his dirty diaper until *Oprah* is over.

12. You have shared a fifteen-minute conversation about your baby with a complete stranger at the grocery store.
13. You filled up your child's baby book before her first tooth appeared.
14. You silently curse people if they call during naptime.
15. You forgot your mother-in-law's first name because you now only refer to her as "Grandma."
16. You arrange your travel itinerary based on McDonald's Playland locations.
17. You are just as surprised when you sleep through the night as when your child does.
18. You consider the person who invented the Sippy Cup a genius.
19. You see a mom from your child's playgroup at the mall and know her son's name but not hers.
20. You consider it a major triumph if you shower by noon.
21. You justify every excessive crying spell with teething.
22. You pick up the phone and call your mother when your baby rolls over for the first time.
23. You have kept your favorite babysitter a secret from other mothers in your playgroup.
24. You have your pediatrician's telephone number on speed-dial.

25. You own the entire *Baby Einstein* DVD collection.
26. You find yourself humming the "Rubber Duckie" song in the shower.
27. You have dressed your baby in whatever is on top of the clean laundry pile.
28. You cry at Johnson & Johnson commercials.
29. You have considered trading your whole life savings for just one good night of sleep.
30. You see your parents in a whole new light.
31. You consider parenting to be the best job in the world.

Angela Jones

To Thine Own Self Be True

By any definition, I am an overachiever and always have been. I was a firstborn, first in my high school graduating class, first in the family to go to an Ivy League school—you get the picture. Once I had achieved some degree of success in my career, I decided it was time to start a family. I prepared for motherhood in the same way I had planned for every other aspect of my life—notes, timelines, to-do lists—you name it, I did it.

Fast-forward to 2004. My sons, now six and eight, were in school full-time and I decided to start my own business as a professional organizer/relocation specialist. Within a year's time, the business grew steadily, and I was adding clients and extra help along the way. Never mind that I was burning the candle at both ends and that the care for my boys, the house, and related activities was being pushed to the limit; I was running a business and feeling on top of the world while juggling many balls.

That is, until I received a wake-up call in June 2005. I had traveled with a client to a retreat for a much-needed four-day getaway. While there, I participated in some workshops during which I was asked what I feared most. That was easy: snakes, heights, ocean liners, sharks, and the like. Then the facilitator asked the question a second time, "Take a moment and really search your heart—what do you fear most?" I literally shrank and sank in my chair. My next answer did not come quite so quickly, nor was it quite so simple. It had been buried deep inside of me for years, protected from any possible unearthing that might occur.

In truth, my biggest fear, something that I was not prepared to say out loud, was that in finding my true, authentic self, I risked losing that which I loved and held dear to my heart—my two boys and my husband. In other words, at forty years old, I finally realized that my angst in life had less to do with creating the perfect life for me and my family and more to do with filling the void in my heart—a product of old, familial wounds. During that moment of realization, I came face-to-face with the possibility that I was truly unhappy with my life—certainly not as a result of an unloving husband or any problem with my two wonderful sons, but as a result of unrecognized, unfinished business.

My lifelong history of taking care of and/or listening to others, rather than nurturing and healing myself, had taken its toll. Moreover, my ability to "fill the void" of my aching heart by creating successes in other areas of my life, rather than listening and paying attention to my inner voice, paved the way to this day of reckoning I had not prepared for. Oh the irony!

And thus began my personal and painful journey of "excavating my authentic self" in hopes of healing old wounds, and in order that I may one day enjoy richer, more loving and intimate relationships, not because the players have changed, but because I have found worthiness in my very existence. These last nine months, while unconventional and inconceivable to most, have been some of the most excruciatingly painful yet therapeutic for me, my family, and friends. My journey is far from over, but I know I am better for having confronted it no matter what lays ahead, even at age forty. Better late than never, I always say. No regrets. No regrets.

Barbara Whipple

LIFE LESSON #1:

Raising a child is one of the most profound things that will ever happen to us. Motherhood is a blessing that can provoke such a change in us that we will never quite be the same. Whether we have one child or several, go back to work, or stay at home, becoming a mother presents us with a myriad of challenges. One of these challenges is the ability to find a balance, as a woman, a wife, and a mom, yet maintain our "sense of self." Sometimes motherhood can stifle our creativity, nudging us into routines that, although necessary for the smooth running of our families' daily lives, may leave us little time to grow as individuals. If we are working moms, we often spend many hours traveling, and our schedules feel even more hectic as we try to juggle our household and children's activities. Single moms will find themselves wearing all the hats in the closet unless they have family close by or a rich support system. And although working outside the home may provide a social outlet, it does not guarantee feelings of personal enrichment.

Alternatively, stay-at-home moms often report feeling isolated by the lack of adult interaction. Increasing in numbers are the moms who stay at home managing the day-to-day running of the family as well as a home-based business. Whether a mom stays at home, runs a business from her home, or works outside the home, motherhood can make us feel as if we have lost connection with our individuality. In essence, becoming a mother is a completely new and different experience, an incredible roller-coaster ride with some consuming stressful lows that at times overwhelm us, as well as the joyful poignant highs that we will deeply cherish for the rest of our lives.

Busy moms live in the demands of the moment. We need to find the missing shoe so everyone can leave and go grocery shopping, then make it in time before the dry cleaners close; keep our doctor's appointment and swing by the pharmacy on the way home; put dinner on the table while helping with homework; and get all the kids into the bathtub and ready for bed so we can do the same! There just does not seem to be enough hours in the day for us to run a household, remain compassionate and responsive to our family, and nurture our own goals and dreams. That is, if we can still remember them. But staying connected with our sense of self, our dreams and visions for the future, is important. It is essential that we take some time to revisit those aspirations and keep them close to our heart. And, in the process, we must evaluate if we are living a life that embraces our authentic self. Do we live our lives as others expect us to, or are we experiencing our days as our true selves?

Now that we are mothers, we may need to redefine ourselves and our perspectives on life by taking a look at who we were before we had children. How did we previously define our identity? What were our values and philosophies? How did we fill our spiritual cup? Did we think about our purpose in life? What were our goals and dreams? Did we have any? What did our vision of parenthood look like and how did we intend to guide our family on their journey? How did we take care of ourselves after a busy week? Maybe answers to some of these questions are not foremost on our minds while we pick the kids up from school or mentally thumb through tonight's dinner options, but giving them some thought can awaken our spiritual voice. It might seem difficult to pursue the same interests and goals we had before, but perhaps there is a way to keep those dreams and goals within reach, even if we need to take smaller steps toward reaching them. As we strive to get in touch with our "true" self and redefine our being, we need to keep in mind that this is an ongoing process; we are always changing, learning, and growing; therefore, our identity will also continue to evolve. When focusing on our life goals, it is essential we stay in tune with our values and philosophies to help us live an authentic life. This is especially difficult when others around us disagree with our thoughts and decisions, and we may feel judged. It is vital that we get comfortable in our own skin and be okay with who we are—not everyone is going to like our choices, and that is okay! We can sometimes "fall into the life" that others expect us to live, and before we know it, we eventually truly lose our sense of self. To avoid this, we need to enhance our self-awareness so that we can experience our days filled with genuine beliefs and principles, then ultimately we may feel more happy and complete.

So perhaps when our child is sleeping, when our husband or a babysitter is helping us, or before we go to bed one night, let's take the time to put pen on paper and outline some core values and philosophies as we embark on the journey to redefine ourselves and create a path for life goals. This alone can empower us and offer a new frame of reference for our daily routines, and who we are as human beings.

Questions to Ask Yourself

- Are you leading an authentic life?

- If not, what steps can you take to get closer to achieving your true self?

- Did you have a vision of motherhood prior to children?

- How does your life currently reflect that vision? Was it realistic or not?

- How did you define yourself before you had children?

- How do you currently define yourself?

- Do you have clarity about your identify? What areas are uncertain to you?

- Do you have gray areas that you may need to work out?

- Do you have a philosophy or purpose that guides you through life? Have you created life goals that are matched with your philosophies in life?

- What is one step you can take toward reclaiming your identity?

LIFE LESSON #2

Figure Out
What Feeds Your Soul

It's a helluva start, being able
to recognize what makes you happy.

Lucille Ball

❧ The Other Side of the Door

I'm in the bathroom for, oh, about twenty seconds when the first request comes. It's my three-year-old, Brandon, asking if he may have a cookie.

Through the door I tell him to go ahead, not at all surprised by the swiftness with which I've been summoned. Since first becoming a mother eight years ago, I have come to the conclusion that mothers have no reason to look forward to any amount of privacy.

I finish combing my unwashed hair, wishing I had time to take a shower before going to the grocery store, but my objective today is to get something for dinner and get back home before my oldest son, Austin, gets off the school bus. As I'm tying my hair up into a ponytail (having given up hope of a more stylish look for my venture today), I am summoned once more from the other side of the door.

"Momma! Momma!" It's my two-year-old daughter, Sydnee. *Oh, now what,* I'm thinking as I yank the door open, only to find my dear daughter standing there, her once fresh yellow outfit literally dripping fruit punch and chocolate chip cookie smashed into her hair.

"Ah, geez, Brandon!" I call out to nowhere; I'm sure he is hiding by now. I pull Sydnee into my bathroom and proceed to strip off her saturated clothing and pop her into the tub to wash the crumbs from her scalp.

There always seems to be some sort of crisis on the other side of the door. Whichever door I close, I always seem to be needed, right now, on the other side of it. When I'm in my office trying to pull together a piece for a magazine, it's my husband on the other side of the door, needing directions for mixing our newborn son's formula, or the correct setting on the washing machine for whites or what temperature he should set the oven to for frozen lasagna. Bless him for helping, but please, dear, I'm busy!

When it's late, and all the children are sleeping, and I think I may just have some time with that dear, sweet husband of mine, I'll no sooner close the bedroom door when suddenly I have a child on the other side, with a fever or a tummy ache or monsters under their bed.

Today I found myself wishing for a door that had no other side. I could close it and achieve perfect peace, perfect quiet, perfect solitude. I could close that door and not have to think about what was lurking on the other side of it, because there would be nothing. Oh, to hear myself think. . . .

The phone rings on my nightstand. "Oh, what now!" I say out loud as I scoop a naked Sydnee from the tub and carry her dripping body into my room.

"Hello!" I say into the mouthpiece with a little too much "What do you want?" in my voice.

"Is this a bad time, dear?" It's my mom.

"No, Mom. Just the usual times, you know. How are you?" I feel a little guilty about the way I answered the phone, but she lets it go. She tells me she was just calling to let me know she'd baked a strawberry-rhubarb pie and wanted to invite the kids and me over to enjoy it this afternoon. I tell her I'd love to, but I've got to get to the grocery store, help Austin finish a school project, get dinner on the table, and between baths, bedtime, and getting the neighborhood newsletter ready for printing tomorrow, my day was already overfull. "Well, dear, my door is open if you change your mind."

I hung up with Mom, her words burning tears in my eyes. I remember being her little girl, whining at her closed bathroom door, needing her and not understanding at all that mothers need some space. Now her door was open, and she was standing in the doorway, hoping that I would come dashing in. It was then that I realized one day I would miss those little fists pounding on my door, demanding my attention.

I wipe my face, dress Sydnee (again), find Brandon's shoes and pack a bag with diapers and bottles for baby Ryan. There's no hope now of making it to the store before the bus arrives, so I load the kids into their car seats for the short drive to Austin's bus stop. As Austin climbs into the minivan, he asks me where we're going. I tell him, "We're going to Grandma's."

Cheryl Mills

❧

LIFE LESSON #2:

As busy moms, we are frequently focused on "what's next?" When responding to a call for "soul food," a little self-reflection may be needed, and then get back to "what's first?" Initially, we need to reflect upon what type of things will rejuvenate our spirits and bring harmony to our lives. While the drama of life can consume us, keeping things in perspective may be a talent that we have to learn gradually. Becoming more aware of our stressors and contemplating how to feed our souls may take us back to the question about whether we sometimes put too much "on our plate." Some of us may have the ability to run on high energy, thriving on the adrenaline charge and intensity of an extremely full day, while others may need to approach life at a more leisurely pace to maintain their equilibrium. If all the people in the world were the same, it would be a very dull place!

Before we had children we may have loved to seclude ourselves at home with a good book in front of the fireplace, but now we might prefer to walk in the mall—alone. Even our belief systems may have potentially changed now that we have children in our lives. What was important to us once might now seem trivial; having a family changes our perspective. And our values and philosophies or visions and goals may all factor into the equation when seeking balance and discovery of exactly what will nourish our souls.

So how do we feed our souls? It's a continuous process, a different way of regarding our daily lives and the quest for happiness. Nourishing our souls may not make life problem free, but it can provide nourishment, add depth and value, and cultivate feelings of well-being for ourselves and our families. There are many different ways to satisfy our souls that can bring joy into our lives and keep us that much closer to our heart center. One size does not fit all! Due to our own personal life events and experiences, each of us will reach out differently to enrich ourselves.

Our own children will offer us an extensive menu to feed our spiritual hunger. Motherhood, with its ever-changing demands, can throw us into a chaotic spin one day but captivate our hearts the next. We take the plunge into motherhood with an unspoken promise to love absolutely and the vow to protect forever, no matter how many terrible twos or teenage tantrums we endure. Our children can disarm, charm, and astound us, from their first dimpled smile to some simple endearing thing they may say or do. We are proud; we admire their endeavors and conquests and encourage them. We fall in love with every artistic endeavor they offer, whether we wear it or hang it, and champion all their strengths and passionate efforts to achieve their best. Our children are embedded in our hearts and feed our souls daily!

Another important avenue that will feed our souls immeasurably is to take time to talk with others. Whether with our spouses, family members, or friends, conversation can help us feel calmer and more connected with the outside world, and boost our energy levels while giving us an opportunity to share thoughts or vent feelings. Behavioral studies have shown that women under stress release a hormone called oxytocin that encourages them to tend their children and gather with other women.[1] The "cuddle hormone," as it is sometimes called, has a calming effect. Consciously seeking verbal connectedness with those who surround us can open many doors for expressing thoughts, and help relieve worries and anxieties. So, in essence, chatting with our friends or other moms and nurturing our children can be extremely therapeutic!

In addition to striving to reach our authentic self and life goals, establishing rituals or traditions may make a profound difference. For example, lighting candles, playing our favorite music, getting a manicure, enjoying family gatherings, or participating in religious customs are all possibilities that can provide comfort and rejuvenation. Many forms of exercise, such as briskly walking with our stroller, or the more calming practice of yoga and meditation before we go to bed, can help us regroup and soothe our souls. We can feel relaxed and incredibly invigorated by taking in nature by the beach, noticing the shapes of clouds in the sky, or listening to the rhythmic crash of waves on the shore. Perhaps the completion of a particularly difficult project at home or work will fill us with a sense of satisfaction and renewed enthusiasm. Allowing ourselves time to journal, recording spontaneous thoughts, or reflecting upon all the things we are grateful for in our lives might also offer a new perspective to our reality. The possibilities are endless—we have been blessed with being busy moms!

Internally reflect upon the question, "What feeds my soul?" Even taking the time to write down some thoughts is a step in the right direction. Once we have identified what will feed our souls, taking baby steps to act upon our answers is next. As our children gradually become more independent, we will have more time to focus on nourishing our souls, and the baby steps will become giant strides!

Questions to Ask Yourself

- What made you smile or laugh this past week?

- What did you feel good about this past week?

- What kinds of things make you feel most relaxed or exhilarated?

- Is there something in particular you feel passionately about?

- What contributed to your most challenging moments in the past few months?

- What could have helped you during those challenging times?

- What types of situations frustrate you the most?

- What thoughts or ideas do you think may help with these frustrations?

- How are your life goal visions congruent with ways you "feed your soul"?

- Who can help you find nourishment?

Ideas to Feed Your Soul

- Write down some of your favorite places to visit—the beach, park, or favorite store. Put the ideas in a fishbowl, and whenever you need a boost, pull out an idea.

- Music can feed your soul—dig out some of your favorite CDs and have a feast! (Do you enjoy different artists/songs for different moods?)

- Think about ways to satisfy your creative side.

- As mentioned in Essential Ingredient #1, identify the types of physical activity that help you to relax or energize you.

- Remember some of the tastes and smells that feed your soul with fond memories.

- Do certain colors or clothes make you feel differently about yourself? Keep in mind that blues tend to be powerful, greens tend to be supportive, and reds/pinks tend to be a signal to celebrate.

- Recall the last time you heard or experienced something that had a profound meaning in your life. Take a minute to write about it.

- Be true to yourself and revisit life goals that might enrich your path and feed your soul.

LIFE LESSON #3

Clarify Future Goals

A good plan is like a road map;
it shows the final destination and
usually the best way to get there.

H. Stanley Judd

❧ Every Spare Minute

One of our team members here in the Community Mental Health Service in the northeast of Scotland is Catherine Clarkson. Catherine worked in a local hospital as a ward sister until she had her little boy, Jason. Catherine's husband was in the military and so he was overseas, sometimes for quite long spells. Cathy gave up her job when Jason was born, but once he was around three, she began to study for qualifications so she could move into the mental health area.

When Jason was five she worked on a part-time basis. This allowed her to drop Jason off at school and pick him up again in the afternoons. In the next few years, Cathy did an open learning course to get further qualifications. She was allowed some study leave, but mainly she had to fit in her studying around her job. By this time, her husband had left the forces and found a job locally. She was happy, in that they were now back to being a family again, but it had meant quite a drop in his salary. To help cope with this, Cathy came to work full-time.

This meant using the school babysitting service to look

after Jason until she finished work around 5:00 PM. It also meant he had to eat his meals at school, and quite often, she found it difficult to get away for sports days and other special events in his school life. She sometimes ended up in tears when he would say over dinner that something special had happened, "All the other mums were there, why couldn't you come?"

Cathy began to feel that she was missing out on some of the most important parts of Jason's young life. She sat down with her husband to discuss options for changing the course their lives were taking. He worked quite long hours, and it was even more difficult for him to get away.

"In a year or so from now, I won't have to miss anything. I won't have to be the only parent missing. I wish I wasn't now," she said, and then burst into tears.

Mike sighed and hugged her, "I know; I know why you work so hard. You are doing three jobs, Cathy—working full-time, studying hard, and running the house, as well as trying to spend every spare minute with him. Jason is only six and he doesn't understand any of that."

Cathy lay awake all night, wondering if she should settle for what she had—a job where maybe now and then she could get time off to go to the school, or take him to parties and spend time there with him. She balanced that against the fact that it would always be important to him that she was there, and if she passed her exams, she would be able to pick and choose.

She prayed for help, and that help came very quickly—but not in any of the forms she had suggested it might! A week later she was leaving a client's house and walking to her car when she saw the mum of one of Jason's classmates.

"I wanted to tell you that I have just started a part-time job. I used to be a nurse, and now I am helping out five mornings a week," the lady informed her.

Cathy nodded politely and was about to go on until the woman added, "I was scared to tell my son that he would have to have lunches at school, that sometimes I would have to work afternoons and not be able to pick him up. I got the courage because of the things Jason said about you to the class."

"About me?" Cathy said in surprise, "What things about me?"

"Didn't you know they were asked to talk about what their parents did? Jason said what your husband does and then he mentioned you. He told them how you go to people's houses and heal the sickness in their heads. He said that sometimes you couldn't come and pick him up on time, or be at different sports things, because your sick people would get very upset and might end up in hospital. He said it was good that you helped them and one day they would be well again!"

Cathy felt tears run down her face as she stammered, "Jason said that about me?"

The lady frowned at her, "Oh, I've upset you; he seems so proud of you, I thought he would have told you."

"Sometimes he says that all the other mums except for me were at different things. I tried to explain why I couldn't be there, but that I am studying, and in a year or so, it will all be different."

"Well he must have understood part of what you said!" the woman said.

It took Cathy nearly two years to finally get clear of her exams and other commitments, and she got more pay and dropped her hours a little. She made sure that she was always available for whatever Jason wanted—school sports days, award presentations, and so on. Walking through the park with him one day when he was nearly nine years old, she asked him, "When you were little and I couldn't make it to your special days at school, didn't that hurt? Didn't you feel let down? You can tell me now."

He looked up at her, "Yes, I was crying about it one day when Daddy came into my room. He told me all about the work you do, how proud he was of you, how so many people needed you and how much you loved me. He said I should be proud of you too and be happy that every spare minute you could, you would always spend with me. So, I understood!"

Cathy slipped an arm round him and confessed, "Well, none of it would have been possible without your dad putting up with my working and studying, sometimes having to make his own meals. Lots of mums are busy. Your dad never complained; he always just encouraged me, and that's why I love him so much!"

Jason smiled, "I know, I hear you telling him every morning!"

Joyce Stark

❦

LIFE LESSON #3:

After taking some time to consider how we may have been reshaped by motherhood, and having reconnected with how we can feed our souls, it is also helpful to determine or clarify future goals for ourselves and our families. We may feel that we are already pulled in many directions on a daily basis, but the act of creating goals and targets for ourselves is fundamental to maintaining a healthy balance for our well-being. By taking some time to think about a long-term vision for our lives, we can often gain the motivation and insight to work on short-term projects that will improve our productivity and bolster self-confidence.

Our life goals may revolve around our family, career, attitudes, hobbies, and health; enhance our integrity/character; or involve ways that give back to the world. Our achievements can offer a perspective that may shape or guide our continued decision making, while providing insight on the areas in which we require more knowledge or discovery. This process can also help identify the deeper reasoning behind our need to conquer certain challenges. Honest evaluation of a goal will help us understand why we aspire to achieve it, which in turn can fuel our perseverance. As our children grow older or as we mature, our goals and ambitions may change, reflecting personal growth.

Exploring our long-term goals initially may seem difficult. However, engaging in short-term goals, for example, doing some research or taking a class in the area that incorporates our future vision, is a step in the right direction. The more short-term targets we set and reach, the less anxiety and stress we will experience. It can also help improve our confidence and increase our motivation and daily achievements. Our brain produces dopamine, a neurotransmitter responsible for feelings of pleasure when we achieve one of our goals; dopamine then further activates the brain to pursue new challenges.[1]

So, if we start with some overall concepts in different areas of our life, such as education, job/career or spirituality, we will be able to back into the short-term requirements that are needed to begin the journey to fulfill our life plan. It's surely our intention that our entire family will be happy and healthy. And, we may ponder about financial budgeting and security in retirement. To achieve these and other goals, we will need to adopt a lifestyle that will increase our odds of success by establishing new productive patterns or eliminating unhealthy ones. These particular examples are goals without a deadline, an ongoing philosophy or way of life that will touch on many aspects of our daily existence with our families. If we are committed to a healthy lifestyle, the food we eat and our approach to physical fitness will most likely be priorities. If financial security is a long-term goal, we may give some thought to our careers and create a plan for our spending and saving habits. Establishing a long-term vision that we truly believe is realistically possible will help us be focused and more organized when determining current and short-term goals.

All our goals are important to us, but as busy moms we may have to "shelve" some for the moment. Writing them down offers the ability to prioritize which ones we are able to work on today, allowing us to revisit and gain encouragement or redirection on others, if we find ourselves lost in the daily grind of life. Reviewing our intentions periodically will also provide the option to change or reaffirm the directions we may choose and affords us the possibility to check our course and measure progress.

Partially achieved or failed goals are an opportunity to learn lessons, adjust our efforts, acquire more skills, and reevaluate whether our expectations are unrealistically high, or if we have challenged ourselves enough. We need to remind ourselves that trying something new will often open doors that would otherwise have remained closed, even if we don't completely accomplish what we set out to achieve. If we set a goal such as saving $100 a month, and can only manage to save $800 by the end of the year, we have still saved more than if we had not set the goal at all.

While it's not a good idea to try and change everything in our lives at once, breaking down our desires in the different areas of our lives can help us set short-term goals. For example, if we want to have a more orderly home, we might make a plan and try to organize one drawer at a time. Taking incremental steps to begin the journey of a thousand steps can be incredibly encouraging. Deciding on a system to keep our kids' rooms more organized, whether it's baskets or hampers, and then rewarding ourselves and our children for following through can help everyone stay focused. Once again, the overall idea is an ongoing lifestyle plan that will come together gradually, even if it takes some time to establish. By combining some organization skills with prioritizing and goal setting, we will experience a better sense of control over our busy lives, which will help us manage stress. Hopefully, once our new systems are in place, we will feel a little more relaxed and have more opportunities to nourish our souls and achieve some of our dreams. Remember, a little chaos may result from wanting to change the order of things, but out of that chaos a new order is possible.

Tips to Organize Your Goals

- Try the "Rocking Chair Meditation." Project yourself thirty years ahead. What, if anything, might you regret not attempting to achieve?
- Think about the life you intend to live and what actions you will need to take in order to accomplish these aspirations.
- Specifically identify areas of your life, such as career, quality of life, or health, and decide what you will need to change or acquire more knowledge of to achieve your life plan.
- Create twenty-year, ten-year, five-year, one-year, six-month, one-month, one-week, one-day tasks and steps that you will need to take in order to reach your long-term goals.
- Make sure your goals are attainable. It might not be possible to run a marathon one year from today, but a two- or five-year goal could be realistic.
- Only focus on one or two large projects at one time. If you would like to organize your entire home, unless you can hire some help, schedule cleaning out one drawer a week, or one closet a month. By taking

smaller steps to achieve your goal, it will be more attainable, and you'll have a better chance of success.

- Create specific and measurable goals to achieve within a set due date.
- It's beneficial to figure out your long-term goal first before breaking it down into daily, weekly, monthly, or yearly goals.

Examples of Long-term Goals

- Live a healthier lifestyle (including a more organized life).
- Have financial security.
- Go back to school and get an MBA; write a screenplay.

Examples of Monthly Goals

- Make a "pampering" appointment (e.g., manicure, massage); make two date nights.
- Pay bills on time.
- Save a certain percentage of your income for retirement.

Examples of Weekly Goals

- Connect with a friend, exercise twice a week, create time to journal.
- Clean out a drawer.
- Do research on MBA programs; read twenty pages of a book weekly—such as how to write screenplays.

Examples of Daily Goals
- Stand up straight—improve posture, eat fruits and veggies.
- Open and sort today's mail.
- Hug your spouse and kids more often.

Now it's time to write out your plan! Also, don't forget to add annual goals, ten-year, twenty-year, and more if necessary. Make sure they are on the path of your overall life-long goals.

LIFE LESSON #4

Make the Bold Move—Make Time to Feed Your Soul

Throughout life, we get clues that remind us of the direction we are supposed to be headed . . . if you stay focused, then you learn your lessons.[1]

Dr. Elisabeth Kübler-Ross

🌸 My Pride and Joy

$CaO[s]+2HCL[g]$? $CaCl2[s]+H2O[l]$

It's all Greek to me, Annette Micek thought miserably as she sat at the kitchen table paging through her new chemistry textbook. *I'll never understand any of this,* the St. Edward, Nebraska, mother of four despaired, fighting back tears.

More than twenty years after finishing high school, Annette had taken the plunge and enrolled at the local community college. "Make us proud," her husband, Casey, had encouraged just that morning as she dressed for her first day of class.

"I'll do my best," Annette promised, but already she was worrying, *Am I really up to this? Have I made a terrible mistake?*

"Follow your dreams." That's what Annette always taught her children, Jonah, Noah, Isaac, and Ashley. But it was a lesson Annette herself had learned the hard way.

Growing up, Annette had always wanted to be a nurse. "Just like you," she told her mom and grandmother, who were both nurses.

"It must be in my blood," Annette said the day she got her acceptance letter to nursing school. But after only a semester Annette lost sight of her dream and dropped out.

Just for a year or two, she told herself. But then Annette got married and started a family, and there was never enough time or money to go back. Instead, Annette worked four days a week as an office manager at a nursing home, ordering supplies and updating personnel files. *So close and yet so far,* she'd pine as the nurses scurried busily back and forth just outside her door.

Diapers and T-ball, bicycles and Sunday school—the years flew by, and in the blink of an eye Ashley was midway through her senior year of high school. "If you don't do it soon, you may never get the chance," Annette's sister, Anita, also a nurse, urged.

"I know," Annette agreed, but the obstacles seemed insurmountable.

Isaac was thirteen, but Noah and Jonah were five and four. *With Ashley going away to college next year, I'd have to hire a sitter,* Annette figured. But she'd also have to quit her job, and with the mortgage payments and other bills . . . and now there was college tuition to think about, too.

But just the thought of Ashley going to college brought a smile to Annette's face. Ashley was a wonderful daughter—generous and loving. And now she was about to leave the nest, stretch her wings, and fly.

It doesn't matter if I never get to be a nurse, Annette decided. *I can help make Ashley's dreams come true. I'm her mom. That's my job.*

"But I don't know what my dreams are," Ashley said as her mom helped her pack for college.

"That's one of the reasons you go to college," Annette explained. "You try different subjects until you find something you really love."

Ashley had chosen Midland Lutheran College two hours from home because that's where her dad had gone. "I'll miss you guys," she said, as she hugged her brothers goodbye, and even before her dad had carried the last of her things into the dorm, she'd set out framed pictures of her family to keep her company.

Ashley cried when it was time for her folks to leave. Later, she took a long walk around campus. She passed the gym and athletic fields where her dad used to play on the football and basketball teams. She'd thought these places would make her feel closer to her family. Instead they made her miss them even more.

Tomorrow's first day of orientation—I'll feel better then, Ashley told herself, but the next day she felt even lonelier and out of place. Until finally . . .

"She wants to come home," Annette told Casey, hanging up the phone. "She's so upset—I said we'd come right away."

"I won't neglect my education—I'll enroll in community college," Ashley told her parents during the drive home. Then suddenly it struck her. Ashley knew how much her mom had always wanted to be a nurse. "Why don't you register, too?" she asked. "We could go to school together. And I'll be around to help with the boys."

Annette felt like she'd been handed a marvelous gift—all she had to do was unwrap it. "OK, I will," she said quietly.

I can't believe I'm really here, Annette thought, standing in front of the school her first day of class. But by the end of the day her spirits had collapsed.

"What's wrong?" Ashley asked when she discovered her mom sitting at the kitchen table.

"This," Annette sniffled, showing her the chemistry book. "It's too hard. I'll never learn it."

"Sure you will—I'll help," said Ashley. "Remember? I got an A in chemistry just last term."

Annette's nursing clinicals started early, so Ashley scheduled her classes for midday. "This way I can fix breakfast for Noah and Jonah and drive them to kindergarten and preschool," she explained.

"Lunch at the student union?" Annette invited when she spotted her daughter changing classes, and by the time they got home Casey had already fixed dinner.

"I'll do the dishes, Mom," Isaac offered. "You and

Ashley have a lot more homework than me."

But one night Noah curled up in his mom's lap. "I don't feel good."

"He's running a fever," Annette announced after tucking him into bed. "I'm sure it's just a bug, but I'll have to stay home tomorrow, maybe take him to the doctor."

"No way!" Ashley jumped to her feet. "I only have history class tomorrow, and I can copy the notes from one of my classmates. You have a chemistry test. The teacher won't let you make that up."

A few nights later, Annette danced through the door, waving her chemistry book—"I passed!"

"Go easy on that book," Ashley smiled. "Next year I have to take chemistry. By then you'll probably be able to help me study."

On graduation day everyone cheered as Annette crossed the stage to pick up her diploma with Ashley right behind her. "It's only because of you I'm here today," Annette told her daughter.

"You said once that God has a plan for everything," Ashley reminded her. "That must be why I came home. God wanted me here for a reason."

Today Ashley is a junior at Wayne State College. "This time I was ready to be on my own, and now I have a dream of my own to pursue," says the active twenty-year-old, who is studying broadcast journalism.

And thanks to Ashley, Annette, now an RN, cares for kidney patients three days a week at a local dialysis clinic. "Everyone has dreams," she says. "I was lucky—I also have a daughter who helped mine come true."

Heather Black

As previously appeared in
Women's World magazine

LIFE LESSON #4:

How do we know when our soul is sending us a wake-up call? When our body is hungry our stomach growls, and we may feel cranky or low in energy. Satisfying physical hunger is a daily need. When our soul is in need of nourishment, the signs may not be quite as apparent. We might find that we are not as available for our family. We begin taking little "internal vacations" during the day, wishing we were somewhere else, or simply experiencing a "feeling" that we cannot quite explain. Our life circumstances may be comfortably familiar, mysteriously chaotic, or a random event may trigger self-reflection and the urge to stop, look around, and become more aware. We must take the time to "listen" to our soul's voice when it calls. Although it might begin in a gentle whisper, if we do not respond, the volume will gradually increase until we have no choice but to stop and pay attention.

Now is the time to start thinking about all the different options that come to mind when searching for ways to feed our soul or set goals, and consider which of them are most valuable at this point. Writing them down in order of preference or prioritizing them will help. Taking the time to identify which activities resonate more with our soul and its needs, or pondering the reality of our limitations, may cause us to reprioritize and simplify the list. Those of us who are mothers with young children might find sleep is the first item on our list, as we are typically unable to sleep uninterrupted through the night. Although it's difficult to find the time, we know that taking naps is extremely important to sustain our energy and maintain the stamina to keep up with our little ones' demands, as well as nourish our own being.

Some of our hopes and goals may seem overly ambitious and cause us to doubt the likelihood of achievement; that's why we need to *simplify, prioritize,* and *be flexible.* Consider the top three items on the list. One of our ultimate goals may be to live a healthier lifestyle. We may want to exercise for an hour a day three days a week, but we could begin with fifteen minutes and gradually increase momentum. It is far easier to build on an established routine and extend time allotments, because if we are overzealous with our expectations, it can cause us to give up. If we truly believe in our hearts that something is important, we will find a way to make it happen, even if in baby steps. If exercising for a healthier lifestyle is an activity that will feed our souls, it will also be a lifelong commitment. So in the broad vision, missing days here and there will not matter; the overall desire will remain strong, and each day and week will bring new opportunities to fulfill our intention. Remember, "Rome was not built in a day!"

Our lives as busy moms are constantly changing, and to keep up, we will need to adapt, simplify, and prioritize, frequently making compromises along the way. It's all too easy for us to become entrenched with our families, children's activities, and the upkeep of our households or careers. But if we don't take some time out for ourselves to recharge our batteries, we will begin to feel like we're running on empty. Assigning chores to older children, sharing playdates, and carpooling with other moms, or enlisting some other form of babysitting help can let some of the air out of the tires and provide a little "wiggle room" for us to schedule time for ourselves.

The next ingredient takes an in-depth look at becoming more organized with all the activities in our homes by creating a "Master Calendar" so that everyone is on the same page. It can help us look at our busy lives from a different viewpoint when we prioritize the daily tasks and activities along with rejuvenation time for ourselves. When we schedule a business meeting for ourselves or a dental appointment for our kids, we put it on our calendar. Similarly, we need to allocate time for our "soul-nourishing appointments" on the calendar in order to have a better chance of keeping our goals. We can go and see a movie with a friend, get a manicure or go to the gym, or we can utilize this precious time to invest in our long-term goals, whatever they may be! Let Dad and the kids fend for themselves—they will survive!

In order to take care of our children and spouses, we must take care of ourselves. This might seem extremely challenging, because we often feel that our days are already way too full! Some of us may remember when we had our first child; the thought of having another one seemed like "Mission Impossible." But gradually, in the natural cycle of life, when we practice some flexibility with perseverance, things somehow come together. Now it's time for us to apply our resourcefulness yet again and "create" some time for ourselves.

Our children will become more independent soon enough as they attend school, engage in extracurricular classes, or spend more time with their friends. Although finding the time to feed our souls may be limited, eventually we will have more opportunities to attend to our life goals and continue to make greater progress toward experiencing the balanced lives we have always dreamed of living.

Organizing Tips to Make Time to Feed Your Soul

- Look at your daily routine in a different way. Make a list of all the regular chores or activities you do and create "windows" of time, however small, for yourself.
- When you calendar various daily activities, calendar your "soul-nourishing appointments."
- Have your spouse or babysitter care for the kids so that you can have time for yourself.
- Make a date with a friend and her children—being able to share and laugh can lighten the load.
- Ask yourself daily, *what is the single most important thing I can do to nourish my soul today?*

"Do you Barbara, promise to keep an organized house with a master calendar and update to-do-list?"

KEEP AN ORGANIZED HOME

Don't agonize. Organize.

Florynce Kennedy

LIFE LESSON #1

Have a "Home" for the Key Items in Your House

Good order is the foundation of all things.

Edmund Burke

Mommy's System

I looked around at the mountains of boxes and my stomach knotted up. I rolled my eyes when my son climbed up on one and knocked over my box labeled "pantry." Rice spilled all over the floor; the white bits looked like maggots had infested our new house. This was our second move in one year, and I thought my head might explode as I assessed the mess.

I took a deep breath and said a prayer. I believed that if God could help Moses part the Red Sea, surely he could help me get organized. I made my way, emptying one box after another, but my concern was maintaining order once everything was neatly put away. Like a day that has a rhythm, a morning, an afternoon, and a night, I too have a rhythm and certain rules that I live by that have helped me achieve this. Being organized keeps me from feeling overwhelmed by household chores. I may not have discovered a cure for an incurable disease, but I have discovered one important ingredient to keeping balance in my life—I have discovered a system.

I have certain duties that I do every day: make beds,

unload dishwasher, touch up bathrooms (I live with three males, so you know the drill), at least one load of laundry so it doesn't get backed up, and I fold my husband's boxers as soon as they come out of the dryer. That way he is only a drawer away from clean underwear, and that makes us all happy.

I try not to overwhelm myself with everyday housework. Every other day when I'm not running the boys to baseball or soccer practice, not doing all those mommy duties, I sweep. Once a week, I give the bathrooms a good cleaning and dust. I mop the floors and clean out the fridge. No one wants to go for that luscious piece of chocolate cream pie only to grab last month's moldy meat loaf.

Everything has a proper place: food in the pantry, videos and DVDs in the entertainment center, underwear in the underwear drawer. I try to put things back as soon as possible.

In the evening, to save time the next day, I skip television games. I'm not very good at "fill in the blanks" anyway. I turn my attention to more important duties, like packing lunches and cleaning up the kitchen. I load the dishwasher, and after it's done, I put the dishes away at night. It helps keep the next morning running smoothly, especially when I can reach into my cabinet and pull out my son's favorite Tonka toy cup. I'm his real hero the rest of the day.

There are little things I do to help maintain order. I keep

my spatulas and serving utensils stored in two silver buckets next to the stove, so everything is easy to find when I'm trying to balance a hot plate of spaghetti and find a scoop so I can dig into the meat sauce pot. In my mudroom we have several hooks hanging up for keys and coats, so we can grab what we need and get out of the house. After my husband accused me of losing his mail (later he found it crumpled up in his jacket pocket), I bought two envelope holders that sit beside my desk. One is for my husband's mail and the other is for bills, dental appointment reminders, and so on. All junk mail is immediately thrown out. I have a box above my desk that I throw receipts into. A magazine holder sits in my study, and every other month I purge. Any good recipes or articles are ripped out and stored in folders labeled "articles" or "recipes." Speaking of folders, I have one filing cabinet for important medical papers, insurance papers, and so on. Last but not least, I purchased several small plastic containers from the dollar store. They sit next to my televisions and hold our remotes.

I don't even sway from my system when it comes to my two boys. The little critters are prone to mess, like I'm pulled to that clothes rack that reads "70 percent off" at the mall. They just can't help themselves. When the kids come home from school, I eagerly line them up, marching them like we're in a parade, over to the coat closet, pointing for shoes in the shoe rack and book bags to be hung neatly on hangers. Hats and gloves are stored in a basket.

One bin of toys is allowed in their rooms. The rest of the toys are in the basement (if you don't have a basement, then one section closed off designated for "toys only" or even a large closet will do). They are responsible for their rooms, although I'm usually there to lend them a helping hand or offer suggestions.

I keep one plastic bin full of crafts. Again, the rest are stored in the basement. This way, when little Mark or Luke is inspired to paint a masterpiece or color a picture for me, they have all their art tools just one cabinet away. Magnet clips are kept on the fridge so I can show off their artwork when neighbors or friends come over. Next to the fridge, I keep a chalk and bulletin board with a calendar on it, writing in important dates or reminders. Before I head out, I take a look at it to make sure I haven't forgotten anything.

A friend once told me that if you don't use it in a year, lose it. So once a year I go through the entire house. I start in the attic and make my way down to the basement. I look at the stuff I've collected over the year and make the crucial decision, like if Aunt Clara's salt and pepper shaker is worth keeping or if I should give it to another deserving soul who might proudly display it on their kitchen table. And what about those size four slacks I promised myself last year that I would be able to fit into? Really now, do you think after forty-three years and two kids I'm really going to get back into them again? Off they go to Goodwill.

Anything used for special holidays (extra dishes, glasses, or utensils) is shelved in the basement or put into storage. My little Christmas elf dish sits perched at the top, eagerly waiting to be pulled out for another festive holiday.

The best thing about my system is that my days are less stressed, and I'm not plagued with endless housework. This gives me more time to spend with my husband and two precious boys. And that is worth more to me than any perfectly neat house.

Terri L. Knight

LIFE LESSON #1:

It's hard enough as busy moms trying to get out the door with our kids—but not finding our keys, umbrella, or certain items that we need when heading out can drive us crazy! A "home" for our basic items can make all the difference when we need them in a moment's notice. And, a home for key items can help significantly with keeping our households in order.

On a personal level, whether we're organized or disorganized, this can translate into a metaphor for how we feel internally. Organizing our homes and lives can provide us with a sense of control on an emotional level and benefit us on a daily basis. Here are some organizing tips on how to create a "home" for these essentials.

KEYS—maintain one spot for all keys in the house and *put them in the same place every time.* It may be helpful to label all the keys for your household such as "garage," "pool gate," or "back gate." Also, if you consider color coding your keys, it can make them much easier to find when you're rushing about.

MAIL—keep up a daily routine, even if it's sorted at night. Use an in-box for mail when you first bring it into the house. Even if you don't open your mail immediately, keep a daily spot for your spouse, your kids, and yourself. Using an inexpensive cardboard box sorter is a quick and easy way to control the incoming mail. The family mail station can also accommodate flyers announcing store sale dates, stamps, envelopes, scissors, and a trash can. And remember, your much-loved junk mail needs a "home" too—don't let it grow out of proportion. Rip up what you're not interested in or shred it in the recycle trash to protect against identity theft.

JACKETS—consider creating a hook for each family member. You can also teach your kids the responsibility of putting their jackets back on the hook each time. Sometimes you need more than just a hook for coats. If your teens have band practice, it's helpful for them to keep a "drop zone" for their instrument, homework, and lunch bag. Many families have actually installed "cubbies" that look like first grade lockers, with a hook for coats and shelves for books and boots, which can help keep kids organized.

MARKET LIST/MENUS—place an "ongoing" marketing/grocery list in a place that's accessible for the entire family. Consider keeping menus in a binder with plastic sleeves or in files and label them, such as, "Chinese Food," "Mexican Food," and "Kids' Favorites."

FILING SYSTEMS—while the number of home offices in the United States has risen by 69 percent, the amount of paper usage has also proportionately increased. Remember the last time you couldn't find a copy of an important document such as last year's taxes? It probably got buried under landslides of catalogs and old school rosters. According to Dr. Richard Swenson, the average American will spend one year searching through desk clutter looking for misplaced objects.[1] To stop the endless cycle of misplacing paperwork, put all documents in one specific location AND keep them in order for easy access. When turning your "piles" into "files," you want to be sure that your files reflect the way you think (which is different for everyone).

For those of us who attach the word "dread" in front of "filing," a solution to fend off indecision and perfection can be found in the acronym TRAF. Organizing paper guru Stephanie Winston states that we only have four choices for every piece of paper we own: T=toss, R=route, A=act, and F=file.[2] As an example, if we receive a flyer for a special store sale, we can T=toss the flyer if we don't really care for the store; R=route the flyer to a family member that might like the store; A=act on the flyer—write the date of the sale on our calendar; or F=file it. If there is a coupon attached to the flyer, we may want to file it until the store sale.

Finally, a rolling file cabinet or expanding file may be useful for storage and retrieval of documents. After purchasing labels, manila folders, and hanging folders, you need to separate documents into piles that will be filed by categories, such as household, medical, or taxes. And you can even organize using a color-coded filing system. Whatever system is used, a habit of filing completed paperwork at least once a week can bring enormous relief to your home environment.

TOYS/PERSONAL ITEMS—encourage ALL your family members to clean up after themselves (even toddlers) by creating a "home" for their toys and items used. For those of us who have school-age children, it will be helpful to teach them to gather their items the night before, such as their backpacks with all their essential items already zipped up. Then put the backpack in the same location every time to eliminate last-minute scrambling.

MEDICINE CABINETS—can contain some of the most "mixed-up" personal items. A regular smorgasbord of old nail polish, prescription and nonprescription meds, or first aid items both new and expired may be found in the family's medicine cabinet. If this sounds too familiar, take time and toss out this repository of old vitamins, prescriptions, cold remedies, and stale nail polish. Group like items together: bandages with first aid items and cold remedies with similar medicines. Also, consider keeping sections or a small bin for the medications of each family member in the cabinet (and out of your kids' reach). Another idea is to color code the medications with a large dot or write their names using permanent markers with each family member having their own color.

REMOTE CONTROLS—how often do you experience complete frustration when you can't find the darn remote control? The solution: keep a "home" for the remotes and make sure all family members know where to return them every time! Something as simple as labeling each remote (for the TV, DVD player/stereo) and then storing them together in one decorative basket will do the trick.

When finding a "home" for your key items:

Step #1—make a list of the items that seem to vanish into thin air!

Step #2—prioritize the items in the order of importance.

Step #3—attempt to find a "home" for the item; if it doesn't work, no problem—try it a different way until you find what works best in your home.

Step #4—let your family know of the new "homes" or locations of items. Then request that they store these key articles in their new homes.

LIFE LESSON #2

Create "Systems" in Your Home

It is best to do things systematically,
since we are only human, and disorder
is our worst enemy.

Hesiod

✿ I Need a Bigger Fridge!

"I think it is time to buy a bigger refrigerator!" my close friend said. She fed her fussy toddler cheese cubes while I reached in to get the milk to pour into our steaming mugs of tea.

"Why?" I asked, looking inside the seemingly spacious interior. A 36-inch-wide Sub Zero seemed to hold plenty for a family of four. "Oh! Are you thinking of having another baby?!" I exclaimed.

"No, two's plenty! What I really need is more space on the outside, to put up my essential reminders!" I saw what she meant. The entire surface was a cluttered mess, covered with calendars, church contact lists, diet tips, her son's sports schedules, babysitter instructions, preschool phone tree, her husband's work contacts, favorite recipes, beloved snapshots, and more, all held to the metallic surface by a mishmash of magnets. This paper explosion obviously contained lots of critical information, intended for quick reference, but it was in such a hodgepodge, she probably could not find anything quickly or easily.

"Remember last week when the toilet was clogged and

overflowing, and I couldn't find my favorite plumber's business card on the fridge for the life of me?" I nodded. "There I was with the baby crying, frantically waving the plunger over the toilet like a magic wand not knowing what to do. What a nightmare! If I had more space on the fridge, I would've had a place to put the plumber's number!"

"Speaking of the potty," she muttered, and scooped up her toddler. "Phewy, I think I need to change somebody's diaper!" She excused herself to the upstairs' changing station for five minutes. I took advantage of her absence to wave a magic wand of my own!

When she returned to the kitchen, her white fridge was nearly empty and shining, cleared of all the lists, with only the cherished photographs on proud display. "What happened?!" she said, worried and alarmed, "Did you throw my papers out or hide them in a drawer? You know that doesn't work for me, pawing through piles. I must have everything out in the open where I can see it at a glance!"

"And you do!" I reassured her as I opened an over-the-counter kitchen cabinet door with a flourish. Her mouth dropped when she saw what I had done. Armed with just a roll of clear tape and a few minutes, I removed the tangle of notices from the fridge and posted each list to the inside of the cabinet doors. I carefully grouped the school lists and her son's sports schedules together inside one door. Recipes and diet tips went inside the door above her favorite counter work space, by the sink, where they would be easy to glance at while she was cooking. In fact, each door had a "theme" to mentally organize it, making the placement of future notices easy and logical.

I placed the contact lists inside the cabinet directly above the phone, so that the tiny numbers were right at eye level for effortless reading. She loved that now she would not need to fetch her reading glasses each time she needed to make a call. At that level she realized that she could see the numbers quickly and accurately. "Now I don't even need LASIK surgery!" she mused. "Wow, I never thought of putting things on the inside of the doors. You are a genius!"

That was a few years ago, and my friend has easily maintained the "hidden" system to the present. She switches out schedules as new ones come, and she has added a pencil, "Velcroed" to the kitchen calendar, which is inside a cabinet that the whole family can reach, and update as needed. Best of all, I have become the family hero, her husband says, as everyone knows where to find all the information they need, and they all stay organized! And I am happy to report that they did get their favorite plumber to fix the toilet after all.

*C. **Lee** Cawley*

LIFE LESSON #2:

We busy moms are constantly on the go to meet the needs of our families and keep our homes in order. As noted in Essential Ingredient #1, we are essentially the CEOs of our households, with multiple projects and players! *Forbes* magazine states that each American spends four hours weekly cleaning and completing household chores; two hours picking up dry cleaning, returning videos, and other errands; fifty-one minutes behind slow-moving cars and in traffic jams; twenty-seven minutes waiting for our kids to show up; twenty-four minutes standing in lines to make purchases; and twenty-three minutes on hold waiting for someone to pick up the phone.[1] Creating "systems" in our homes can reduce stress and help everyone experience a higher level of productivity, calmness, and ease.

Implementing systems can also help our households run more efficiently and promote greater communication among family members. Creating an action plan and engaging our family by soliciting their feedback may increase the odds of their participation to keep a more organized home environment. Below are organizing tips and suggestions on implementing "systems."

MAIL/NEWSPAPERS/MAGAZINES—many of us may have piles of mail stacked up, newspapers scattered throughout the house, and piles of cascading magazines lying around. Referring to the previous Life Lesson, finding a home for our mail is essential, and it is enormously helpful to have one location for newspapers and a separate one for magazines (possibly each person in the home having their own designated spot). Magazines, newspapers, and flyers pile up quickly, so picking one evening a week or month to sort through our stacks can make a difference. Also, clipping out favorite recipes and interesting articles not yet read provides space for our new magazines and newspapers.

A routine for junk mail, newspapers, and magazines is one system that is missing for most families and seems to cause the most frustration. We may collect various magazines with similar titles because we sometimes align our identity with these publications. For example, after completion of culinary school, we changed careers but still want the publication. This yearning may cause us to collect cook books, magazines' food sections, and recipes from the newspapers. We may never intend to read these space hogs, but keeping them around reminds us of what we once were—or what we still want to become. We may truly benefit by creating systems for these items.

"MISSION CONTROL CENTER"—most family communications tend to occur in the kitchen, the "mission control" area of the home. This also means that telephone calls, messages, notes, and family meetings take place in this part of the house. If the kitchen is not your main "assembly area," choose a room where the most activity takes place. If the kitchen is your choice, it is helpful to first clear the counter space of ALL unnecessary items— creating a clutter-free zone. If the counter is overloaded with unused cookware and kitchen gadgets, consider donating these items to a charity or finding an alternate location for storage. For example, a great storage idea for flat, oversized serving plates is wrapping the plates in a secure clear bag and storing them under a guest bed. Relocating such items frees up valuable kitchen "real estate" for items we use on a regular basis. When the extraneous is out of the way, we are ready to create a family system.

When effectively organizing the home, many families use a to-do list (detailed discussion on using to-do lists is covered in Life Lesson #4 in this chapter), a message board, a telephone pad, a master calendar, and magnetic clips for messages or coupons. The main item that will be used for daily activities and upcoming engagements is the master calendar (detailed discussion on using a master calendar is covered in Life Lesson #3 in this chapter). Because we juggle so much throughout our day while we are raising our kids, purchasing a large planning calendar for the wall can help the days run more smoothly. A family meeting once a week to review our master calendar can help prevent missing a meeting or a special activity, or double-booking a time slot with different activities. During the family meeting, any new scheduling from the master calendar should be added to our own personal calendar and vice versa. We can also slot upcoming discussions on vacations/holidays such as planning to visit family members. To make this part of the meeting enjoyable for our kids, let them (if old enough) write in the new schedules and appointments that pertain to their activities. This task can give our kids a sense of involvement and help them feel vital to the "family team."

For those of us who own and use a computer, calendars, schedules, and to-do lists are often available in software. But if a computer or purchasing additional software is not in our budget, or we simply do not want to use it to organize electronically, there are other alternatives. The items that we need are available in most office and discount wholesale/retail stores at an affordable price.

Another system to consider that can have a profound impact is a messaging system. The suggested items to use are an erasable whiteboard, magnetic clips for messages on the refrigerator, and a pad by the phone. Although advancements in technology make it easy for many to own cell phones, the messaging center is also vital in communicating our whereabouts at any time of the day. The key to success in the messaging system is habit. When writing down on the whiteboard that we are shopping, or keeping a rule for our kids to jot a note with a phone number so we can reach them, we are not only showing security and concern for each other, but we are passing on a sense of responsibility. It is important to take time in our family meetings to explain what's necessary and make sure that each family member understands the system.

MARKETING LISTS—posting a marketing or grocery list for all family members to use can save time and help us remain organized. Even our school-age children can add to the list. It doesn't mean we have to buy a particular item, but at least we'll know what our children want or believe they need. Also, it may be helpful to have a rule that the person using items that are running low, such as the last carton of milk, box of crackers, or package of cheese, must write it on the marketing list.

Creating a list can also stop us from spending too much money. How many times do we enter a supermarket without a shopping list? Running out to purchase a carton of milk may be an exception. However, when we need two or more items from the market, that's where temptation can exceed necessity. Stores are extremely savvy in placing products that we may not need, but still purchase on compulsion.

Many of us busy moms feel that quickly going up and down each aisle will give us the benefit of not forgetting an item. This technique may cause us to "cave in" and buy the treats that we purchase only on special occasions. If we take a shopping list, the coupons for any of these items, *stick to only what's on the list, and shop after we've eaten a meal,* we are more likely to spend less money and buy only what's necessary.

With regards to organizing tips for coupons, instead of throwing them all into a drawer, consider putting them in separate envelopes or clipping them together by topics, such as baby items, toiletry items, and groceries. In fact, using a mobile coupon organizer can allow us to grab the grocery list and run. We can scan for usable coupons while waiting to pick up our kids from school.

When creating systems in your home:

Step #1—make a list of what is not working.

Step #2—prioritize the areas in the order you want to tackle them.

Step #3—attempt to create the system that needs revamping. If it doesn't work, try a different way until you find what works best for your family.

Systems for the Holidays

Consider deciding on a theme for the holidays. A theme allows families to focus and can guide in gift giving and budgeting. Themes can also unite families and stimulate creativity. Here are examples of possible themes for the holidays and suggestions for gift buying and giving:

- "Red Christmas"—create everything in red, such as foods, decorations, gift wrap, and wardrobe accessories.
- "Chanukah Attitude is Gratitude."
- "International Holiday"—celebrate the holiday in the style of another country's tradition.
- "Religious Verses"—create a theme around a verse and let this passage guide you for the season.
- "Relax and Read"—purchase books to give for gifts. Almost everyone has some type of book they like to read, whether it's fiction or "how-to" manuals in print. This theme minimizes time spent shopping while looking for a meaningful gift.
- "Get Certified"—gift certificates are increasingly popular for the most challenging person on our list. Places such as their favorite coffee shop, bookstore, or even movie tickets are a few ideas of where to look.

Systems for the Holidays (cont'd)

- Shopping online is one of the fastest-growing services, as it's not only buyer friendly, but buyer convenient.
- Make sure to put yourself on the gift list—a massage or a facial may do wonders for your hectic holiday pace.

Systems for Gift Wrapping

- Set up a temporary gift wrap station; cut sheets in advance. Keep plenty of tape and tags on hand.
- Stay with one color theme; that way, any ribbon, bow, paper, or card will match.
- Hire your babysitter, house sitter, or housekeeper to help wrap.
- Purchase inexpensive fabric and use to wrap up gifts. This is a quick and creative way to wrap, and it's reusable.

Time Tips for the Holidays

- Delegate tasks to others and APPRECIATE the work they perform. It may not be the way you would like it, but not everything can be done if only you do it.

Time Tips for the Holidays (cont'd)

- Create a list of babysitters and contact them in advance about their holiday schedule.
- If we love the holidays, then we should take the time to enjoy some moments to ourselves by asking others to assist in laundry, cooking, and the daily chores.

Tips for Holiday Cards

- Consider sending cards online.
- To bring back a warm and connected feeling, consider calling friends and family with holiday wishes, rather than writing them.
- Look for ways that your children can participate, such as assigning your teenager to display the holiday cards and your eight-year-old to help seal envelopes and apply stamps.

LIFE LESSON #3

Keep a Master Calendar in Your Home

*I see something that has
to be done and I organize it.*

Elinor Guggenheiner

❧ The Wondrous Whiteboard

Girl Scouts, Boy Scouts, sleepovers, dentist and doctor appointments, birthdays, PTA, swim meets, football games, working late, weddings, funerals, and birthday parties. You get the picture. Now, my family is certainly not involved in all of these activities at once, but at one time or another, all of these items have applied to us. Why don't we throw in who's washing the dishes, who closes the gate and garage, and who rides shotgun? Well, our family found a simple solution that, although not foolproof, provides a little sanity and clarity to the wild runaround that being part of an active family entails.

Yes, it's the Wondrous Whiteboard. It's a simple, framed magnetic whiteboard that measures about 12 x 15 inches. It's not even on the wall, just propped up on the kitchen counter where we can access it readily and make additions when necessary. You will also need whiteboard markers. We have ours in a drawer close to the board. (*Important note:* Do not by any means store any permanent markers in the same drawer. We learned this the hard way. Do you really think your kids—or you for that matter—are going to check to see what kind of marker you are using before writing?) And to wrap it up, get some clever magnets that your kids can relate to. We have baby pictures in a magnetic frame as well as James Bond–themed ones for my son and Frida Kahlo, Che Guevara, and Diego Rivera for my Latina Pride daughter. They are kept on the fridge and put on the board as needed.

The calendar part is simple. Every Sunday night after dinner, we bring the calendar and markers to the table. We note the days of the week—let the kids do their thing with colors, then the dates. And we fill it in. All appointments, special events, out of the ordinary errands, you get it. The point here is to have no excuse for "I told you I had a party at my friend's house tomorrow night!"

"Sorry, son, it's not on the calendar." So your week is out there for all to see—no excuses.

An added bonus in our home is the solution to the "she washes this week not me" dilemma. In our humble home, yours truly (the mom unit), does not wash dishes. Hey, I bring home the bacon and do most of the cooking (they do help, but I am the main chef). And, trust me, there is nothing that bothers me more than the old "it's not my turn" routine. Here's where the magnet comes in. The magnet that is on the Wondrous Whiteboard for the week represents the person in charge of washing the dishes. Just that simple. Two kids: one washes, one dries (my children so resent my proud proclamation to anyone that is listening that I have two dishwashers, two gardeners, you get it). An added bonus is that whoever washes the dishes gets shotgun in the car. Remember calling shotgun all the time as a kid? No more fighting over who sits where. The "backgun" person is in charge of opening and closing the gate and garage as well.

I may not have solved any major world conflicts here, but let me tell you, the arguments I have been able to bypass with the Wondrous Whiteboard are well worth a minor investment of time and money.

Shotgun!

Natalie Orta

✣

LIFE LESSON #3:

Busy moms are typically the gatekeepers in the family. Our spouses check with us to find out what's happening on a certain date; the kids ask if they're allowed to attend various functions; and we are continuously scheduling appointments, such as with a dentist or doctor. In other words, our lives revolve around times, dates, appointments, and activities. And it feels *horrible* when we realize we've missed an appointment, especially one that we've waited on for a long time!

Using a master calendar for our challenging schedules can transform our lives. As discussed in the previous chapter, a calendar for all engagements is necessary to keep the family's activities running smoothly. When purchasing a master calendar, consider the following: a larger numbered family needs a larger calendar. It may sound obvious, but when we think of everyone's activities within our family, especially with school-age children's schedules, a wall-size master calendar will work best. When writing in the activity, we may want to use various colored pens for different family members. Our son may want a blue pen, while our daughter wants a purple one. Let family members pick out their favorite pen colors. This will make "master calendar" night more fun, especially for younger children. The use of designated colored dots for each family member on a chart (next to the calendar) makes it easier to identify and differentiate everyone's activities. To avoid confusion, it may be a good idea to use the same colors previously assigned to each family member if using a "coding" method with medications.

As discussed earlier, pick one night a week for a family meeting to review the following week's activities. Perhaps a Saturday morning works well for the entire family instead of an evening time. Whatever day and time we choose, it's best to stay consistent and make it a priority to ensure the "family meeting" takes place. Reviewing the current scheduled items and making the necessary additions together as a family helps everyone stay on the same page. Our organized actions can also teach our children worthwhile habits, which can carry through with them as they mature.

Make sure to add birthdays, anniversaries, school holidays, and other special times to the calendar. It's better to know about occasions ahead of time so the family can prepare accordingly.

A master calendar not only serves as a tool for planning daily activities, but can give us insight on how we are scheduling our time over the long term. Perhaps a monthly review shows tendencies of "overscheduling" on particular days. If we find there are not enough days for family members to have time off to relax, we may reconsider our commitments. Time to unwind is just as important to schedule as doing the shopping or picking up the dry cleaning. Also, as overbooked busy moms, we tend to deprive ourselves of the self-care needed to stay replenished. As discussed in Essential Ingredient #1, learning to say "no" to various projects and requests will help bring much-needed relief. Consider asking ourselves, "What can I delete from my day today?" Over time, the ability to achieve greater balance in our lives will hopefully be reflected on the master calendar—the art of balancing our active lives, along with time to unwind, and magically becoming more organized!

LIFE LESSON #4

Prepare To-Do Lists
with Updated Priorities

Nothing is so fatiguing as the eternal
hanging on of an uncompleted task.

William James

To Do: Laugh at Self

As a mother of two very young children, I have learned that it is the small victory that separates a good day from a bad day.

The other day, for example, was a good day. With my trusty to-do list in hand, I remembered to bring my car in for service (check), juggled my daughters, their car seats, and accompanying "stuff" in and out of the loaner car without losing anyone (check), and dodged numerous meltdowns, my own included, along the way (double check).

The following day, however, did not start out as promising. Instead, I awoke to the realization that my beloved to-do list had let me down. It seemed that it could only help me remember the things I thought to jot down. Unfortunately, I was getting good at forgetting almost everything else.

This time, it was my stroller. Upon opening my eyes that morning, it occurred to me that I hadn't retrieved it from the loaner car. Apparently I had been too busy congratulating myself for spying a Sippy Cup at the last minute that had rolled underneath the passenger-side seat.

Consequently, I now had a new task to add to my to-do list: drive back across town to reclaim the poor, abandoned stroller. And though it was still early, my hopes of turning the day around were overshadowed by the growing number of things I had forgotten in recent days and weeks—like the infant car seat carrier I left at the door of my daughter's preschool. I remembered it only after I had gone through the time-consuming process of coaxing her away from the playground, around the rain puddle, past the climbing tree, and back into the car, all while carrying her baby sister, only four months old, on my other arm.

Or the day I left a bag of diapers in the checkout aisle of the grocery store. Having no choice but to take my daughters to the store during the "witching hour," I was so determined to get in and out that I simply forgot to grab the bag after paying. More mystifying yet was the gallon of milk that I left at the same grocery store in the exact same manner only a few days later.

Yes, by that morning, not even a to-do list could save me. Forgetfulness had become a major theme in my life, and I was not taking it well.

A card-carrying type-A personality, overachiever, perfectionist and, at least according to those who love me most, control freak, I could take a lot of the chaos that motherhood had thrown at me, but not this. Forgetfulness was worse; it was personal.

Chaos was an eternally cluttered house, severe and never-ending sleep deprivation, or a crying baby who needed me at precisely the same moment as my potty-training preschooler—stressful, maybe, but at least somewhat under my control. Forgetfulness, on the other hand, felt entirely out of my control. It represented a personal betrayal of my brain cells, and I feared I might never recover.

It was in this haze, lost in my thoughts over the deteriorating state of my mental faculties, that I pulled into the preschool parking lot and ran into another, more veteran preschool mom. Given her tenure over me, I trusted her to suitably commiserate on such matters as my recent forgetfulness, which is why after telling her about my recent failings in self-pitying detail, I expected a much different reaction than the one I received.

I expected her to reassure me, preferably in a soft voice, using words like, "I know, I know . . . it's okay . . ." Even an empathetic "it must be hard to be you" would have been nice. Instead, she took one look at me, as I shifted the heavy infant carrier from one hand to the other while trying to grip my other daughter's hand, school bag, and stuffed animal with the other, and laughed. Heartily.

Eventually, she stopped laughing long enough to fill me in on a time-honored truth of parenthood. "You're not alone," she said, "Everyone's brain turns to mush when your children are this young!!!"

"Everyone's brain turns to mush?" I replied in a high-pitched screech, keenly aware that my challenges were not as unique or life altering as I had allowed them to feel.

"Yes, of course!" she exclaimed. And though her words were full of the reassurance I so desperately needed, it was her laughter that popped the protective bubble around my self-indulgent reverie. It was her laughter that invited me to laugh along too.

Interesting strategy, I thought to myself after leaving the preschool parking lot on my way to reclaim my lost stroller. After all, I may have been embarrassed when a grocery store employee chased me down in a crowded parking lot with a jumbo bag of diapers, but even my daughter had been able to laugh. Afterward, she kept pointing at me, giggling and repeating, "Mommy, you forgot the diapers!"

Maybe if both a veteran mom and my own daughter could laugh at my memory's shortcomings, I could learn to do the same. *It sure beats feeling sorry for myself,* I thought with a laugh, as I rescued my stroller from the dealership and heaved it back into my own car.

I made my way back to the preschool, and decided that the day didn't have to turn out as bad as I initially feared. Maybe I just needed to reprioritize my to-do list. Surely, remembering to laugh at myself was a good place to start.

Chrissy Boylan

LIFE LESSON #4:

While a master calendar serves us well for various functions and appointments, we know that it's the power of to-do lists that reminds us what to bring to the function, what to ask at the appointment, or what to buy at the store. These lists can free our minds of chaos: all the errands we need to run, the e-mails we need to write, and the phone calls we need to return. As busy moms, we typically complain that we can barely remember today's day or date and feel as if our brains are turning to mush! The simplicity of to-do lists can make a tremendous difference.

As stated in Life Lesson #2 of this chapter, to-do lists are essential. And nothing feels better than checking off finished items or errands. But what about the monthly or annual items that need completion? What about the leaf-filled gutters around our roof with the promise of unseasonably heavy rains? Or changing the filters for the heater and air-conditioning unit to ensure they continue to run efficiently? Keeping "reminder ticklers" is not only helpful, but can eliminate future potential problems.

Many of us have certain items that never seem to get crossed off our to-do list. If we look closely enough, we may find that procrastination might be the key. One possibility is that we feel it will take forever to complete a project, so we keep putting it off. Another scenario is that it may generate a certain emotional feeling that we would prefer not to experience; therefore, we continue to stay away from the task. Or, we can analyze the heck out of it, and then realize that we're simply just so busy that a particular task isn't a priority.

Any schedule could drive the most efficient mom crazy if not written out daily. Moreover, it's also helpful to remind ourselves to prioritize and maintain flexibility on a continuous basis. Remember: *Most lists are not 100 percent finished by the end of the day.* We need to move up what is required and "bump off" what can wait for tomorrow. And the items "bumped off" may or may not become priorities the next day, but we should continue to list them so we don't lose sight of them. When we encounter a task that seems too big, such as packing for a family trip, consider taking baby steps and avoid perfection at all costs. For example, these steps may consist of: (1) write out a packing list for each family member two weeks in advance; (2) pick one evening per family member to pack up their needed items a handful of days before the trip; (3) let our older children pack their own bag with adult supervision; and (4) write down last-minute items that need to be packed for each family member, such as medications or our child's favorite stuffed animal for bedtime.

An additional thought to consider is to actually take

certain items from our to-do list and place them on our own personal calendar. Some moms take it one step further and write in the time of day that the task will be completed. It may sound a bit crazy, but scheduling errands or tasks could be the most productive way to complete them. The busy moms who experience days so utterly full often say that they get more done when they are insanely busy because they know they must make time for tasks, such as running errands and returning phone calls.

On the following pages, templates are provided that can be used for daily to-do lists, weekly chores, and an annual to-do list. We suggest enlarging the forms on a photocopier for your use. **If you would like free, downloadable to-do lists for your planning, please log on to www.biobinders.com and click on the tab, "Chicken Soup for the Soul."**

Tips for to-do lists

- Whether you are a morning person or a night owl, complete your to-do list the night before or the first thing in the morning, when you are the most alert.
- Keep the list handy and portable. Out of sight is out of mind.
- Continue prioritizing throughout the day.
- Stay as flexible as possible. When raising kids, you never know what's going to happen next!

DAILY TO-DOs

Name: _____ Date: _____

It is suggested you complete this the night before or first thing in the morning each day.

✓	To Do	Comments
___	_____	_____
___	_____	_____
___	_____	_____
___	_____	_____

✓	To Call	Comments
___	_____	_____
___	_____	_____
___	_____	_____

✓	To E-mail	Comments
___	_____	_____
___	_____	_____
___	_____	_____

WEEKLY CHORES

This form can be used for each family member. For kids, you may want to consider putting star stickers at the end of each day or week after they've successfully completed their list. If it's not a daily chore, it may help to circle the day it should be completed, then check it off once finished.

Name: _____

Week _____

Example:

(check off when completed)

	Sun.	Mon.	Tues.	Wed.	Thurs.	Fri.	Sat.

Name of Chore

	Sun.	Mon.	Tues.	Wed.	Thurs.	Fri.	Sat.
Take Trash Out	—	—	—	—	O	—	—
Make Bed	—	—	—	—	—	—	—
Vacuum	—	—	—	O	—	—	O

Name of Chore

	Sun.	Mon.	Tues.	Wed.	Thurs.	Fri.	Sat.
_____	—	—	—	—	—	—	—
_____	—	—	—	—	—	—	—
_____	—	—	—	—	—	—	—
_____	—	—	—	—	—	—	—
_____	—	—	—	—	—	—	—
_____	—	—	—	—	—	—	—
_____	—	—	—	—	—	—	—

ANNUAL TO-DOs

Enter Month _____

✓	To Do	Comments
___	_____	_____
___	_____	_____
___	_____	_____
___	_____	_____

Enter Month _____

✓	To Do	Comments
___	_____	_____
___	_____	_____
___	_____	_____
___	_____	_____

Enter Month _____

✓	To Do	Comments
___	_____	_____
___	_____	_____
___	_____	_____
___	_____	_____

SOLICIT HELP

Alone, all alone
Nobody, but nobody
Can make it out here alone.

Maya Angelou

"No Fred, I am not taking a nap!"

LIFE LESSON #1

Learn Why We Don't
Ask for Help

None of us has gotten where we are solely by
pulling ourselves up from our bootstraps.
We got here because somebody
bent down and helped us.

Thurgood Marshall

❀ I Don't Wear That Red "S" Anymore!

Busy, busy, busy. I used to define myself by how much I could accomplish in a day. Activity equals productivity equals "I must be a worthwhile person; look how much I can do!" I took care of my house, my husband, my son, my dog, and my cat. I was involved with people in my church family, my friends, my extended family. I planned the vacations and the birthday parties, and I volunteered at my son's school. I paid the bills, and I took pride in my house looking like it belonged in a magazine—everything in its place and always dusted and decorated "just so," I took care of all the details in life, and in the process I felt fulfilled. I was wearing a red "S" on my sweater all the time in my eyes—"Superwoman!" What I didn't realize at the time was that feeling fulfilled is not the same as taking care of myself.

One day, I suddenly started dropping things for no reason. I had dizzy spells. I thought I was just tired. But as the symptoms worsened, I knew something was wrong. I went to the doctor, and he said that it was either multiple sclerosis (MS) or a brain tumor. As a young mom, I didn't think either one was a great option! Turned out it was MS. My life had to change dramatically and immediately. I was confronted with finding my value apart from my high standards of productivity.

I learned everything I could about MS and how varied the symptoms are. Some people can't walk. Some can't see. My problems seemed to involve weakness in my arms. It's not that I didn't have the strength to lift things, but the transmitters in my brain didn't "tell" my arms that they had that strength. The very next month after my diagnosis, I learned that I was pregnant with my second child. Now I was scared. *How could I possibly care for another baby along with all of my other activities?* This was the catalyst for me to finally give myself permission to not do everything at superspeed! If I was going to be able to take care of yet another soul, I had to learn to take care of myself so that my MS symptoms wouldn't rule my life.

I had to ask for help. I had to accept help. I had to lie down and take a nap in the afternoon to recharge my batteries, rather than folding a load of laundry and sweeping the porch. I had to lower my standards from "perfect" to "good enough." And really, if the dishes are done and we all have clean clothes, that is good enough. I learned that if I didn't draw the boundaries around my energy, I paid the price. My family paid the price. I accepted a disabled parking sticker. I am not in a wheelchair, and when you look at me, my disability is not visible. But accepting this help is vital to my energy conservation in any given day! Humbling myself this way is a hard thing for "Superwoman."

But as I began to take care of myself, and not try to do it all alone, my MS symptoms lessened. I still take care of my husband, my kids, my house, and my life, but I am more choosy about HOW I take care of them. I've seen that I really can't do 230 things and do them well. So I pick my five favorite things and do them as well as possible. Even if there are things that come up that I really want to do, I don't say yes right away. I think about how that activity fits into my priorities. I'm not afraid to say "No, I cannot take on any more right now." When people ask me how they can help, I come up with tangible ways, like asking them to bring me a meal when I know my day will be filled with other things and there won't be time or energy left to cook. When someone asks me how I am doing, I don't answer "just fine" and put on my happy face. I really tell them how I'm doing. I'm tired and looking for some help with—you name it, the project at church, the field trip planning, whatever "it" is. Not all the time. But once in a while, I have found that people really appreciate the blessing of being able to give.

Don't be afraid to let down your standards and accept less than perfect, but good enough. Allow people to help you. Maybe it won't be done the way you would have done it, but it's good enough. And be choosy about where you spend your time and energy. You may not have MS, but you also have only so much energy each day. Take care of yourself first, and the rest of life will fall into place. I don't wear that red "S" anymore. I just can't be superwoman. That's okay. My husband and family still think I'm "super" and so do I. The most important lesson I have learned is that my value doesn't come from what I can accomplish in a day— it comes from just being me.

Pam McCutcheon

LIFE LESSON #1:

We may know mothers out there who maintain the art of balancing their very busy days. These moms juggle their tasks efficiently while they continue to nurture themselves and reach out for support. Although we admire these women for achieving their successes, not surprisingly, there is a huge audience of us who are still in the process of figuring it out. And in the meantime, we might find ourselves over-stretched, struggling to stay on top of everything, and experience a feeling of "treading water" to simply stay afloat.

There are many reasons why we may avoid asking for assistance. A standard reason is that we feel compelled to attain "superwoman" status—capable of doing it all! In this instance, although seeking some help could improve the quality of our life, perhaps our ego or guilt will stop us. Or, we may want things done a specific way and our spouse or others who offer to lend a hand simply don't do it "right." Either way, we might find ourselves "doing over" the already completed chores or spending countless hours in an effort to achieve perfection.

Men are often teased when they avoid requesting directions. We sometimes poke fun at them as they drive around endlessly—determined to find the destination versus stopping and asking for the darn directions. What about us busy moms? Why are we not asking for more help? And what would the picture look like if we did?

To better understand why we may choose to stay away from seeking more assistance, it might be beneficial to pursue a little "soul-searching" and explore a possible deeper meaning. It could make a difference to look back and see if we established this pattern over the course of our lifetime. Perhaps thinking about past experiences when we did reach out for help is another avenue that could shed some insight on our current beliefs. Some of us view ourselves as "failing" with motherhood if we seek assistance. There are so many reasons why we may avoid finding the support we need and deserve.

More often than not, when we consider seeking help, we

think of the practical and physical aspects of it, such as finding someone to help with the kids or assist with keeping our household functioning. However, it's important to stay open to the possibility of needing to reach out on an interpersonal level or even explore the mental health arena for ourselves. While our society continues to make tremendous strides in recognizing the benefits of therapy or medication, a stigma associated with seeking help still prevails.

An article from the American College of Obstetricians and Gynecologists (ACOG) gives an example of when it is necessary to seek support. It explains that, "Roughly 10 percent of new mothers experience postpartum depression in the first year after giving birth," and advises that it's "different from the more common baby blues, which affect 70–80 percent of women. Postpartum depression is more intense and must be present for at least two weeks to distinguish it from the baby blues."[1] Paul A. Gluck, MD, chair of ACOG's Florida section also points out that, "Feeling sad after delivering a healthy baby doesn't mean that you are a failure as a mother," and adds, "New moms need to know that postpartum depression is not a character flaw but a chemical imbalance . . . that responds well to treatment."[2]

Whether it's getting help with our physical tasks, our kids, or addressing mental health issues, the more we talk with other women, the more we learn that we're not alone.

We do in fact share so many similar experiences in the life of motherhood—reach out, ask for help, and you may be surprised what you find out!

Questions to Ask Yourself

• Have I always had difficulty asking for help?

• Are there certain people from whom I'm more comfortable asking for help versus others? Why do I think this is?

• Is my spouse supportive with ways to help?

• What were my negative experiences when asking for help? What were my positive experiences with reaching out?

• Are there certain situations where I am comfortable asking for help versus not asking for help?

LIFE LESSON #2

Learn How to Ask for Help

Remember, if you need a helping hand, you'll
find one at the end of your arm . . . As you
grow older you will discover that you have
two hands. One for helping yourself, the
other for helping others.

Audrey Hepburn

❧ Good Mommy

"Grab her! She's opened the door!"

"What? Where? Which door?" my husband responded to my scream. "She can't do that. We have those slip things on the doorknobs."

"Well, tell her that," I retorted while running with him down the long hall and out the open front door.

"Which one do you want?" he questioned.

"I'll take that one," pointing at our toddler daughter scooting up and around the curve on our street. She was staying on the sidewalk, but her little legs were long and nimble and she was making great time.

Meanwhile, my husband hustled down the hill toward the main street to catch up with our second toddler who was squealing with delight at this new game of "chase" with Daddy.

We caught them but could hardly punish them beyond mild scolding for doing what came naturally. Our beautiful, healthy twin daughters were a blessing after eleven years of marriage. They were also a shock to our lifestyle. My husband was away a lot, but when he was home, it was for days at a time, which was wonderful because he was able to give hands-on involvement on a day-to-day basis. When he was off on a trip, I had my hands full and kept the girls pretty much confined. They spent their time trying to figure out how to break loose. They got pretty good at it.

After our "unscheduled run," I returned to making ice cream and shaping burgers for the grill while stopping every few minutes to help dress our little ones for their second birthday party. We expected guests to come celebrate in just a few hours. I had mountains of work to do before then and wondered why I'd ever invited family and friends with their toddlers and dogs to join us for food and festivities in our backyard. I was tired already and the day had barely begun.

My husband took the girls outside while he decorated the patio, set up chairs, and tried to keep them away from the pool. We had a fence around it, but they tried to wiggle through, over, or under it without any luck. This brought wails of frustration.

My folks arrived with a dog-shaped piñata, which was a perfect diversion until they began filling it with candy, unsuccessfully trying to hide it from our daughters. They had more "help" than they could handle. In an attempt at yet another distraction, we pulled out the paper plates, napkins, cups, and tablecloths. They wouldn't stay on the tables in the breeze and forced us to search for some way to safely tack them down. Meanwhile, the girls decided the tablecloths made wonderful tents and pulled them off the tables and onto the grass before we could stop them.

The custard was ready for the ice cream churn, so I poured it in and packed the tub with rock salt and ice. *They're going to love this,* I thought. It didn't interest them at all. My attempt at a special, old-fashioned birthday treat turned out to be just so much extra work. The neighbors began to arrive and the kids found chasing the old, mild-mannered and, fortunately, friendly dogs around the yard much more entertaining.

The phone rang and I grabbed one of our girls as she was preparing to thrust her hand into the cake while I clutched the phone and listened. A voice began to weep loudly. No need for me to say anything. I knew it was another mother of twins who had come to the end of her coping ability. The Mothers of Twins Club had a hotline for us to call for advice or help anytime, day or night. This was my month to be on call. *Why did I agree to that for this month?* As guests continued to arrive, I held the phone and pointed them toward the backyard. After ten minutes, the voice said, "Thanks, I feel so much better. You're wonderful, you helped so much." Funny, since I never said a word. I didn't learn who the caller was for several months but smiled at the thought that just having an understanding ear was enough to get her through another minicrisis. If I hadn't been the hotline number, I might have called it myself that day. In fact, as I listened to her, I realized just how much I needed to learn how to ask for help with these two busy toddlers instead of trying to be "Supermom." By sharing the workload, I also would be sharing the pleasure.

I hung up and went out to join what looked like utter mayhem, with toddlers, adults, and dogs covering every space of our small yard. The children were sharing toys reasonably well, adults were watching them and laughing together, the ice cream was frozen and ready to serve, and the sun was beginning to get a late-afternoon pink glow. In spite of it all, our party was a success.

Later, after baths and in their pj's, our little ones hugged my neck and said, "Good, Mommy."

"Yes, you're good, Honeybuns."

"No. YOU good, Mommy." And with that they gave me big, wet kisses on each cheek.

My heart was filled with joy. Exhausted? Yes, but it was worth every minute. Busy? That was an understatement. Days were frantic sometimes, frenetic most days, but good and happy. And now, thirty years later, they're still good—and calmer, except for the days we keep our grandchildren.

Jean Stewart

LIFE LESSON #2:

Once we're more comfortable asking for help, we may experience feeling stuck on how and who to ask. Of course, it sounds so basic: pick up the phone and tell a friend or family member we're in need of assistance—but it just isn't always that simple.

For starters, we understand that everyone is incredibly busy these days. Therefore, when we're closer to that comfort zone of seeking help, it's essential to practice asking for help by acknowledging how busy they probably are, and learning how to hear "no" with grace and ease. Of course we're entitled to experience frustration if they say no; however, we need to consider how it's conveyed.

We can set up the scenario with our friends, family members, and coworkers, and state, "I am practicing asking for help." Once sharing we are in practice mode, some may say "yes" more readily, and those who have to say "no" are likely to do so in a gentler manner.

Another aspect for us to think about when requesting help is to explain the specifics as much as possible. When we're specific and brief, it helps others have a clear understanding of what is being asked of them, and it can help them evaluate if they are able to support us with our request. For example, if we recently had a baby and are utterly sleep deprived, the last thing we have energy for is making trips to the market. So, an idea could be to call a few friends that live locally and mention that when they make a trip to the store, to please let us know, in case we need a carton of milk, a box of cereal, or any other food essentials. As a courtesy, make the offer to someone who's in a similar situation as yours—pick up an item for a friend when you're at the market; it's then possible the reciprocation with that person may fall into place naturally.

In addition, many of us may periodically experience days when we feel like we're just in a total rut. This is when we need to be very selective in reaching out. When we're at our most vulnerable, we need someone who we absolutely trust. If we feel like we're just falling apart and possibly heading into crisis mode, we must let our loved ones know. They want to know! We also need to take into account that our loved ones may not be equipped to address certain issues of ours; this is where we need to consider seeking out professional advice.

Another aspect of seeking help may simply consist of wanting to connect with friends due to feelings of loneliness. In the previous Essential Ingredient, it was pointed out that the hormone oxytocin is associated with women gathering with other women. When we reach out to other women for support, it's a tremendous step toward achieving the mission of attaining support.

It's helpful to keep in mind that most people want to help. Reaching out to others makes most people feel incredibly good. Some will even be quick to say, "That's what life is all about, being there for others and extending love."

Questions to Ask Yourself

- How do I feel when someone says "no" when I ask for help? How do I respond to them? Am I understanding or do I express disappointment toward them?

- What approach do I take when seeking help? Am I clear and concise with my request for help?

- Do I reach out and ask for help when needed? If not, what is keeping me from doing so?

- What are a few steps I can take to ask for the help I need?

LIFE LESSON #3

Identify & Enhance
Your Support System

Refusing to ask for help when you need it is
refusing someone the chance to be helpful.

Rick Ocasek

✿ My Miracle

A blizzard raged outside my front window, but it was tame compared to the storm in my soul. *Please, not today*, I thought as I turned on the computer to write in my journal.

"When the weather is icy or snowy I pray the call does not come," I pecked out the words. "I'm scared to death I'll get the call and I won't be able to make it out of the airport. I'm not sure what I would do if I missed my transplant because of inclement weather."

"It's just a rash," I protested the day the doctor told me I have scleroderma—an autoimmune disorder that tightens the skin, attacks joints, and constricts blood flow. "I just need more exercise," I told my husband, Scott, when I started feeling draggy—but it wasn't long before climbing the five steps of our Vestal, New York, split-level left me gasping for breath.

The scleroderma had attacked my lungs, leaving my heart swollen with excess fluid. "Pulmonary hypertension—I feel sorry for you," a cardiologist remarked, and his pity angered me so much, I changed doctors. But I couldn't change the course of my disease, and it was straight downhill.

Over the next year I was in and out of the hospital a dozen times. Doctors installed a portable, battery-powered pump to deliver a constant stream of drugs to my heart and lungs. But my only real hope was a double transplant. That is, if a matching donor could be found in time.

And so the long wait began. My banging heart ticked away the hours, days, weeks, and I grew so weak, I could barely dress myself in the morning.

"Let's use paper bowls for cereal," I told my daughters, Lucy and Emma, because after they left for school I could toss them in the trash instead of struggling to rinse and load them into the dishwasher.

I moved so slowly, a trip to the market could take most of the day. I applied for a handicapped parking tag, but when I saw the expiration date, I burst into tears because it was a year away and I didn't know which would expire first—the tag or me.

"The clock is ticking and I can't help but ask myself, will I get these transplants in time?" I journaled, then dropped into bed, exhausted.

"Let's watch TV," Lucy and Emma piled in alongside me, and later we colored and played games. They kept me smiling. They gave me hope, a reason to fight.

I understood what it must be like to surrender and take your last breath. There were times when I was ready to let go and accept it. But I couldn't give up. I had to fight till there was nothing left—for Lucy and Emma.

"I want to see time pass, watch them grow up and, most importantly, be there for them. I don't want them to grow up resenting the mother they didn't have."

Eventually I needed a wheelchair. Scott had to do all the cooking and housework. But friends, neighbors, and family pitched in—babysitting, bringing meals, dropping by to keep me company for an hour or two.

Our church held a barbecue to raise money for our medical bills. Lucy's dance class put on a big show, and friends organized a walkathon.

"Just more proof that angels are everywhere," I noted in my journal, "and my job is simply to be grateful, and that I am. The power of gratitude is a very intense thing. It warms my soul and gives me an understanding of giving that I never knew before. Being sick has given me the opportunity to really see and understand what unselfish giving truly is. I learn from it, and hope that sometime I will have the chance to be the giver and not the receiver."

One day I sat at the window watching a neighbor stroll down her driveway to fetch the mail. It was such a simple thing, but I felt so envious. I couldn't take my girls for a walk in the park. I couldn't dance or even brush my own hair.

Stop it—right now! I gave myself such a slap. *I don't have time for any pity parties. It may not be much of a life, but it's mine, and I'm going to cherish every day of it!*

I wrote in my journal, "I have promised myself I will

never feel 'the grass is greener.' I will never believe that I am settling for a lesser life, because I know there is so much more. Not only will I take whatever life doles out, but I am going to love it, treasure it, and savor it."

I called a friend and enjoyed a lovely conversation. Later, Scott, the kids, and I watched a funny movie, and I laughed till tears streamed down my cheeks.

"Hop into your pj's and I'll read you a story," I told the girls, and I savored their snuggly warmth and the tickle of their hair on my arms when they leaned close to see a picture.

"We're going out to dinner to celebrate your birthday," Scott said a few nights later—only instead of a restaurant, he rolled my wheelchair into a banquet hall where my friends had gathered to throw me a surprise party.

"I have been in my pajamas for two days. Now that's a good party."

It was 4:30 AM when the call finally came. "We found your new heart and lungs." I didn't shout. I didn't cry. I felt peaceful, ready for whatever God had planned.

The surgery took eight hours, and I barely survived. Internal bleeding. Rejection. Infections. I suffered every possible complication. Two weeks after my transplant, I felt weaker than before the surgery. But I'd come too far to give up now. A thirty-eight-year-old woman from Iowa had given me the ultimate gift. I wasn't about to let it go to waste.

I can do this, I kept telling myself, and sure enough. . . .

"Welcome Home—We Love You!" read the signs that greeted me the day I came home to begin my new life. And what a life it's turning out to be.

I still have scleroderma, but the improved circulation from my new heart and lungs keeps the disease totally at bay. The swelling is gone from my joints. I feel so fit, I'm signing up for dance class. And recently when the city sent me my new handicapped plate, I sent it back because I don't need it anymore.

I never imagined what a blessing it could be to shampoo my daughters' hair, drive them to school, or just carry a basket of laundry to the basement. "Every day, in many ways, we are blessed," I wrote in my journal. "It's our job to realize our blessings are sitting there in a huge pile just waiting to be acknowledged and accepted. It's our job to notice those blessings, treasure them and then share them, so others know that they, too, are blessed."

Heather Black
As previously appeared in
***Women's World* magazine**

❧

LIFE LESSON #3:

Once we are in touch with our need to solicit help, and feel a greater degree of confidence when asking for it, we then can take action. Where do we begin? What is our current support system? Who and what is it made up of? In addition to family and friends, our support may come from our religious affiliations, neighbors, other moms at our kids' school, our work environment, a life coach, or hired help. Once we identify our support system, it is helpful to evaluate it and see if it's working to our satisfaction. And for the areas in our lives in which we don't have adequate support, we need to explore how to enhance it.

It's also helpful to ask basic questions such as, "What aspects of my days are most frustrating?" Or, "What times during the day are most hectic?" "How can my support system be strengthened to address these issues?"

The value of our emotional well-being is another area that deserves attention. In our day-to-day busy lives, we strive to experience the most healthy and emotionally balanced life possible. However, a tremendous amount of energy can become invested in the dynamics of relationships and may consume us. If this becomes a dominant aspect in our lives, as mentioned in the previous Life Lesson, it may be worth soliciting a mental health professional as part of the "team" to enhance our support system. It takes a strong woman to explore old emotional patterns and learn to create new reactions and behaviors. When we take care of our emotional health, it can bring out the happiness that we've always dreamed of experiencing.

When we have successfully created our support network, it is amazing the way it can permeate throughout the family! Now that we are mothers, we tend to appreciate our moms a whole lot more. We may find ourselves asking them, "How did you do it?" Although our mothers typically did not have formal help, what many did have in the previous generation was a stronger sense of community. Our moms may ask us, "What in the heck is a 'playdate'?" At one time, homes and neighborhoods were often comprised of extended families. These days, many of us are quick to admit we barely know our neighbors. We are living in times when we need to create our community and strengthen our support systems. We are the ones who need to make it happen!

Exercise to Complete

- What/Who is my current support system?

- What aspects of my support system are working and what's not working?

- For the areas that are not working, what are specific ways I can enhance my support system?

Latest Trends in Self-Help

The trend toward self-help and recovery books is on the rise as consumers are seeking solutions to feeling constantly overwhelmed. The Center for Organization, www.centerfororganization.com, has coined the phrase—"Suffering from the O-Factor": overtired, overworked, overspending, overweight, and overcommitted. Because we are so out of control, we seek control within our surroundings and ourselves.

LIFE LESSON #4

Consider Paying for Help

There is no higher religion than human
service. To work for the common good
is the greatest creed.

Woodrow Wilson

❧ My Joy, Not My Job

"Waa, waa, waaaaaa," cried two-month-old Micah from the nursery.

"You're not supposed to be awake yet," I whispered, trying not to sound disappointed. "It's only been fifteen minutes."

Bending over the crib to rescue my wailing daughter, I noticed the sheets beneath her bottom were wet. *No-leak diapers—yeah, right!*

"Honey, did you pick up my cleaning?" yelled my husband, Michael, from our bedroom on the other side of the house.

I sighed and shook my head. *I promised! How could I have forgotten?*

"I'm changing the baby," I replied. I needed to buy some time to think about how best to break the news to him.

Baby Micah began gnawing her fist as I slipped the disposable diaper beneath her tiny bottom.

You're not supposed to eat for another forty-five minutes. I cradled my newborn in the crook of my arm and walked to the bedroom.

"I think Micah's going through a growth spurt," I told my

husband. "She's not sleeping much, wants to eat every other hour, and I've changed seven diapers this morning!"

Michael looked me in the eyes.

"You forgot my dry cleaning, didn't you?"

I nodded.

"I would have picked it up myself if you had told me," he said with a sigh. "I don't have anything clean that matches."

I hung my head. "I'm sorry. It slipped my mind."

"I don't have time to pick it up and come home. I guess I'll have to dress at the dry cleaners."

Michael disappeared into the bathroom. "Did you call a housekeeper like we discussed?"

I heard him digging through the clothes hamper looking for something "not so dirty" to wear to the cleaners.

"I know I can do it myself. I just need to get organized." I shouted defensively.

Michael put a hand on my shoulder. "I'm not attacking you," he said, slipping on his shoes. "It's just that, well . . . the baby's too much for you, isn't she?"

Micah began crying. I pushed back my own tears as I sat down in an armchair and let her nurse.

Michael was right, I thought. *Being a wife, a stay-at-home mother, and trying to work full-time from home was overwhelming. It is too much,* I admitted to myself. *I'm doing the same amount of work as I did before the baby, plus taking care of the house, Michael, and Micah . . . It's like having two full-time jobs! No one should have to work two full-time jobs!*

For a few minutes, I sat silently as tears rolled down my cheeks.

Moments later, a thought floated into my mind: *Michael and Micah are your joy, not your job.*

I looked down at my nursing baby. Her face was so sweet. How could I think of her as a chore?

"Well, here I go," Michael laughed as he walked into the living room. He was wearing dress shoes, a golf shirt and sweat pants. "Sorry I yelled at you," he said, as he bent to kiss me good-bye.

"No, honey, I'm sorry that I forgot your cleaning," I replied. "I love you. Have a good day."

That afternoon, I called a housekeeper and enlisted my mother to help with Micah a few days a week. Every time I start to feel overwhelmed, I remember that God gave me a child and husband so I could delight in them. They are my joy, not my job.

Stephanie Welcher Thompson

LIFE LESSON #4:

As it is, many of us live paycheck to paycheck, which creates additional stress in our lives. Even for those who don't carry these worries, many would prefer not to pay for something that we perceive as "extraneous."

One of the main areas that we busy moms may need help with is finding someone to assist in taking care of our children. Whether it's because we're working moms, have a doctor's appointment, or need "sanity" breaks, finding someone who is trustworthy and loving with our children is hard to attain. These days, an available extended family is not typically the norm. Many of our children don't have their grandparents to jump in and help, and we can only rely on neighbors or friends up to a certain point, if that's even an option.

Now is the time to reevaluate our lifestyle and prioritize our spending. As an example, for stay-at-home moms with very young children, paid help a couple times a week can make an enormous difference. Even if it's costly, it could be the best investment for us, our kids, and our family as a whole. We can even look at it as a short-term plan, and then at a later date reevaluate the need for hired help. During the hiring process, it might make a huge difference to seek out someone who has interest in supporting the whole family unit. For instance, someone who is happy to assist with laundry, and whatever else is needed when the kids are sleeping, would be highly beneficial. It is important to list the areas in which we need help, whether it is for ourselves during the day or to provide more date nights with our significant other—whatever it is—staying open to hiring help is important. As mentioned throughout this book, ultimately, we know that when we're refreshed and take the time to nurture ourselves, our whole family benefits.

As discussed in previous Life Lessons, our optimal mental health is a critical aspect of life for our family and ourselves. Whenever possible, we need to avoid putting a "price tag" on this area of life; improving our coping skills and finding the means to achieve ultimate happiness is one of the greatest benefits our family can experience. And we're not only speaking of a therapist or a psychiatrist; there are many additional resources that may help improve our mental health. For example, we can hire a physical fitness trainer, hire a professional organizer to clear out the clutter and bring sanity into our home, or hire a "life coach" to help balance our lives. When we identify the help that we've made peace paying for, it's important to keep in the back of our minds hiring someone who incorporates the philosophy of promoting independence. Avoid becoming dependent on hired help; find someone who gives us the "tools" to maintain successes on our own.

Whether we choose or do not choose to hire support, it

is still an exercise worth exploring. We may end up deciding that paying for help is not the answer, but if it is, we
will have found the means to add a quality of life that a
price tag could never beat.

Exercise to Complete

- What are the current conditions that make it difficult
  to pay for help?

- If finances are an issue, go beyond this. For example,
  consider the value you place on hiring help or the lack
  of it, trust issues, or lack of recognizing that you may
  need help in a certain area.

- Communicate the ideas you are exploring with your
  spouse.

MAKE TIME
TO SLOW DOWN

Oh, give us pleasure in the flowers today;
And give us not to think so far away
As the uncertain harvest; keep us here
All simply in the springing of the year.

Robert Frost

"Mom, I want to be just like you, when I grow up . . . huggable!"

LIFE LESSON #1

Make Time to
Take Deep and Full Breaths

One way to break up any kind of tension
is good deep breathing.

Byron Nelson

ᲐᲢ One Mother's Mantra

I am the proud, doting mother of the Great and Powerful Pudinsky. No, my child is not named after an Eastern European dictator. It's just that our four-year-old daughter, Anna Marie, is assuming full control. These days, she has launched a hostile takeover of our home, unleashing toddler tyranny in ways I never thought possible. Temper tantrums, nonstop chatter, ceaseless requests for candy, and, of course, the infamous twenty-questions game that goes into overtime, or at least until the buzzer (bedtime) rings.

After a hectic day of assisting colleagues at the private university where I work, my tolerance level is whittled to negative one on the "Mommy, I need you now!" scale. Dad is in similar condition on weekday evenings, barely able to wiggle a toe from his perch on the recliner.

Honestly, after a full day of serving and assisting so many people, is it any wonder quality time with family is simply slim pickings? But family time is vitally important, so you've got to squeeze it in somehow.

I have often marveled at the dreaded end-of-the-day

zone. It is the time when I'm most tired, cranky, and hunting for a morsel of sanity, eventually questioning my mothering skills. I have those days; wondering days. Am I the best mother I can be? Is there something more I should be doing? Am I spending enough time with my child? Am I doing the right things? Am I from another planet? Help!

Basically, I give myself a good old-fashioned dose of self-inflicted "working mother" guilt. Here's the upshot—I believe I've discovered a New Age treatment to combat the guilt. Breathe deeply. Hug often. Read books nightly to my child. Laugh heartily at the silly sayings she so proudly announces to her father and me at the dinner table. Rejoice in her innocence. She is a gift. She is my little girl, hair tied up in pink ribbons and bows, who needs her mommy and daddy to play the Memory Game with her every night, to help her do puzzles, to cuddle, read, and snuggle at bedtime so that she feels safe.

I have also noticed that when I take a moment to slow down, so does she. When I sit down on the floor next to her and rest my bones, so does she! It is not always the magic cure-all for a rambunctious toddler, but in my house it seems to be a fine fit.

Here's what I know: parenting is a double-baton-throwing balancing act between the dreamsicles of motherhood and the reality of daily chores, errands, and messes. So, after my daughter has hopped out of bed (again), repeating the nightly dog and pony show (experienced moms know what I'm talking about here!), I realize that she has changed my life. I'm tired, yes, it's true. Yet, after a moment of prayer and reflection, I kiss my daughter on the forehead for the umpteenth time, and smile from ear to ear.

I am still smiling because I realize that happiness is loving her the best I can.

Kimberly Edwina Campbell

❧

LIFE LESSON #1:

We rush to get ready in the morning, take the kids to school, and then head off to the workplace, if we work outside the home. Next, we run to the market, dash to the bank, and hurry through eating lunch because we need to complete some errands before picking up the kids from school. Then we're rushing to our kids' extracurricular activities, scurrying home for their homework, bathing, and eventually getting ready for some shut-eye. Whew— it's exhausting just to read this—no wonder so many of us forget to breathe!

Due to the fact that breathing is spontaneous and automatic, we don't actually need to think about taking our next breath. Therefore, many of us develop the unhealthy habit of taking shallow breaths. Taking deep and full breaths is something that falls off our radar. And the stress in our lives can sometimes cause this unwanted tendency. There's probably not one person who's reading this that isn't aware of the importance of taking deep and full breaths, but how many of us actually do it? An article on the website *holistic-online.com* explains, "Scientists have known for a long time that there exists a strong connection between respiration and mental states. Improper breathing produces diminished mental ability. The corollary is true also. It is known that mental tensions produce restricted breathing."[1] Taking a slow, deep, purposeful breath when we are feeling anxious or frazzled will "pattern" our body back into a calm state, tipping the balance back into our favor.

Holistic-online.com further explains that when our breathing is too shallow and quick, we take in less oxygen and we don't eliminate sufficient carbon dioxide. As a result, our bodies are deprived of oxygen and a toxic buildup occurs, which diminishes the cell's ability to function well. A large part of our vitality is dependent upon the health of the cells in our body; every cell in our body requires oxygen. Deep and full breaths are fundamental to promoting our physical, mental, and spiritual well-being.[2]

When we commit to integrating this important practice into our lives, we need to ensure we are actually taking these deep and full breaths properly. A common tip is that it's essential to breathe slowly through the nose—not through the mouth. In Diane Evans's article for Knight Ridder/Tribune News Service, she notes that JoAnn Herman at the College of Nursing at the University of South Carolina in Columbia finds that there is a difference between chest breathing and diaphragm breathing.

Diaphragm breathing is what we want to strive for. When chest breathing, we increase the size of our chest cavity by pulling up; as a result, most of the air stays at the top of our lungs, which is not an efficient way to breathe.[3] Herman further states, "The diaphragm is the muscle that separates the chest cavity from the abdomen. If you want to know what it feels like to breathe from your diaphragm, lie down on a hard surface and put one hand on your chest and the other hand on your abdomen. When you breathe in, the hand on your abdomen should move out, and the hand on your chest should stay still."[4] Herman also notes that when we do this, the air comes down deeper, which makes it easier for the oxygen to be picked up by the blood vessels. Our breathing then slows down because we don't have to breathe as frequently to maintain the proper oxygen levels.[5]

We know that effective breathing can have a powerful effect on our mind, body, and soul, but many of us don't know the fundamentals of the proper way to breathe. Although the material in this Life Lesson has only a limited amount of information to keep us informed of the powerful impact of breathing, perhaps it will inspire us to seek and learn more. In addition, there are numerous activities that incorporate effective breathing and offer amazing benefits, such as yoga, meditation, and visualization exercises. Below is an example of an exercise to walk us through the calming effect of taking a slow and full breath.

Place your hand palm side toward your belly over the navel. Consciously relax your shoulders and pay close attention to the way your breath feels as it travels down into your lungs. As you inhale slowly through your nose—your hand should be pushed away by your belly while your diaphragm relaxes to draw in breath and your chest gradually expands. Hold your breath for a moment and simply feel your heart beating. As you slowly exhale through your nose your hand will be drawn back towards your navel—your diaphragm contracting to push out your breath. Visualize all the tension in your body and mind leaving with the exhaled breath. This slow deep diaphragmatic breathing will create a wavelike motion with your hand on your navel.

Tips to Promote Effective Deep Breathing

- Make a point of doing it throughout the day—while driving, making dinner, during a shower—it's something you can do any moment of the day!
- Buy a book that incorporates meditation and visualization exercises with the powerful effectiveness of breathing.
- "Interview" friends that do yoga or other activities that promote breathing. Find out how it has made a difference in their lives.

LIFE LESSON #2

Revisit the Powerful Effect of Spending Time with Nature

The richness I achieve comes from Nature,
the source of my inspiration.

Claude Monet

❧ A Rabbit Moment

It has been a fast year. My son's wedding took up much of my awareness. Moving my father into a retirement community occupied more of my time. There were showers for friends' children, bar mitzvahs, new babies. The days flew by, and now it is my birthday again, my traditional time for reflection on where I have put my energies for the past twelve months and what I will do in the coming twelve.

The reflection begins with breakfast. Today I will not have my usual cereal with wheat germ and rice milk but something different, to alert myself to the newness of this time. I toast some multigrain bread and brew a pot of hazelnut coffee, a treat not often bothered with. After a leisurely meal, it is time to get down to business.

I open the back door to throw out the uneaten bread for the birds and halt in my tracks. There is a baby rabbit munching the tips of clover sprouting under the bird feeders. Rabbits always command my attention. I stop whatever I am doing to watch them, to participate in a rabbit moment. I am delighted by the way they nip off a blade of grass and munch it in, like slurping a long strand of spaghetti, or the way their ears shine translucent, backlighted by the late afternoon sun. Even when they are doing nothing much, just resting in the tufts of uneven lawn, stretched out long and flat with only their heads visible like lions in the African plains, I find them fascinating.

I have noticed that no matter how busy I am when a rabbit appears, a rabbit moment has a beneficial effect on my day. It slows me down for one thing. Any fast movements around a rabbit will make it freeze, briefly stopping all activity, and then send it scooting for cover, so I find stillness is the best way to observe. It also has the effect of short-circuiting my runaround thoughts to focus on one thing, initiating a state of mindfulness. And it propels me into a place of awe. I never fail to gasp at a rabbit sighting, to be impressed by the great and profound detail in creation. Rabbits touch my heart even as they eat my tulips.

And eat my tulips they do. Every bud is neatly nipped. There is no tulip bouquet for this birthday, but I am not upset. I have seen a rabbit and it reminds me of what I need to do this year: slow down, focus, and be as aware in the rest of my life as I am in a rabbit moment. I determine to take my time to focus, like my rabbit friend as it eats each bit of clover. I choose to appreciate even ordinary things. Relaxing in the sun. Eating a meal. Doing an errand. And each day I will look for something, even more, expect something to make me feel fully alive. If something as tiny as a rabbit can evoke such joy and passion in me, surely my day must be filled with moments worthy of awareness.

"Thank you, little rabbit," I say softly, "for the wonderful birthday present."

The rabbit lifts its head, swiveling its ears in my direction, and then after seeing that I mean it no harm, continues to munch.

I think I will stop to buy a pot of tulips on my way home today. They will look grand on my table. And when they wilt, I will plant the bulbs in my backyard so that next spring when they begin to bud, the rabbits will be able to feast—as my spirit does in their presence.

Ferida Wolff

LIFE LESSON #2:

When our children are hard at play, they test our limits by typically dismissing the need for a break; whether it's their afternoon nap or the need to refuel their bodies with a snack, our kids may love to play until we "run interference" with them. We know our children's needs. Nature's instincts are to protect our little ones, and sometimes even from themselves!

As busy moms, how many times do we dismiss the need to slow down and reenergize ourselves? From fitness clubs to the latest gear for home exercise, our society gives us a multitude of products and services to relieve our stress. But there is a form of relief that usually does not come with a heavy price tag: the powerful, yet mysterious healing properties of nature.

Yes, nature is a mysterious healer of all kinds. Irma Robbins, in the *Journal of Humanistic Counseling and Development*, quotes Professor Thomason saying, "One of the common Native American perspectives on health and healing has to do with the power of a harmonious relationship with nature," and adds, "From this perspective, life . . . cannot be artificially divided into categories but must be considered with all the interrelationships within nature. Disharmony with nature is unhealthy. Native American rituals are designed to restore harmony and thus health for those who might suffer" (Thomason, 1991).[1]

How can busy moms seek time for nature's revitalization? While the examples are vast, here are some practical tricks that some use to receive the maximum joy and benefits of our natural world.

Nature in Our Own Backyard

Gardening is now considered one of the top recreational activities in the United States. Even if we have a very small plot of land in our backyard, this hobby can take us back to nature; nurturing a bed of flowers or fresh vegetables from seedling to harvesting is a great joy to many. Dean Fosdick sites author Eva Shaw's health plan for nature, and says that "gardeners have a responsibility for getting people back to the soil as a means of coping with pressure."[2] While a morning of pruning weeds and watering plants can give our bodies a thorough workout, the ever-sweet-smelling scent of roses or small orange blossoms can also send both powerful and pleasurable messages to our brain.

Many of us may live in urban areas that offer no land to nurture a small garden. However, if we drive or walk past apartments or condominiums, we will see that residents find room on their compact terraces to grow small trees and flowers. We too can try a hand at giving our terrace an exotic look with plants that suit our "local climate." If the terrace is shady, we need to remember to buy plants that are not sun-loving. And if water restrictions are an issue, try buying drought-resistant plants. These few facts will give us a chance to create a terrace garden with a green thumb.

What happens when we live in an apartment that offers no extra space? Potted plants, flowers, and paintings/photographs of nature can create an intimate atmosphere for a bit of nature. And, if indoor plants are not conducive to our living space, table-size ponds trickling with water over stones may soothe our ears. With a bit of ingenuity, we can sense the pleasure of nature in and around our homes.

Still, some of us do not enjoy the experience of plants and gardens; we might prefer other outdoor activities in our yard. We may live in climates that bring four distinct seasons to our region, yet we've forgotten some of the joyous hours spent jumping in a pile of ruby-red leaves in autumn or building a snowman during winter's first storm. And those of us living on either coast know the powerful effects a sparkling sea can bring to our minds—both an exhilaration and calmness that can revitalize the most tired of souls. Taking time to see the sunrise or sunset can reconnect us with life and nature. Going to the beach for a barbecue and to watch a bonfire or going to the lake and renting a boat for the day are other ways to keep us connected.

Taking a walk can truly connect us with the beauty of the outdoors. The next time we want to see nature, we could say to our kids, "It's time for a nature walk." This stroll might be around the neighborhood or a nearby park that can give us a view of the different species of trees that are in bloom various times of the year. Or how about listening to the different birds singing at a particular time? If we notice the clouds and colors in the sky, listen and watch the birds, and observe the rabbits and squirrels along the pathways, we realize how much truly surrounds us.

A Camping We Will Go!

After an atypical spring season of cold, rainy weather, we may yearn to visit a national park or forest with our family. The country is filled with these marvels, and any region proudly shows off its natural heritage. While some of us can afford the luxuries and accommodations of hotels, many of us need to seek creative ways to enjoy nature's glory—especially if we are vacationing more than just a few days. Even though we love the outdoors, a number of us busy moms do not feel that "roughing it" brings the joy and relief we seek from nature. Our days can be filled with outdoor activities, but our evening accommodations may need to include some electricity and running water. Perhaps we can consider renting a recreational vehicle (RV) for our vacation. While we must take into account the higher cost of fuel before planning an RV trip, these vehicles may still offer many families affordable travel with the amenities of home and "hookups" for electric and water service at specific campgrounds. These sites are usually very economical per night. And if these facilities are somewhat "empty" of vacationers, we may be able to stay overnight for half the price. Always ask.

For those of us who have healthy backs and strong constitutions for "roughing it," or pitching a tent under the starry skies, nothing beats camping in our favorite national or state park. Most campsites have restroom facilities and a supply of drinking water, but only a few include showers. Camping costs still remain inexpensive, usually at a very low cost per night. Here are some quick tips and sites to start planning our nature getaway:

- For a quick glance at the different sites throughout the United States, www.recreation.gov lists all fifty states' recreational facilities and can break it down to the activities available in each park, such as biking, fishing, and hiking.
- AAA offers an "Online Tour Book" with a database for lodging, destination information, and listings of U.S./Canada campgrounds.
- Go online, call, or write the tourism department of any state or province and find out what its region can provide for family vacations.

LIFE LESSON #3

Appreciate the Small Things in Life That Really Matter the Most

The quietest poetry can be
an explosion of joy.

James Broughton

✿ Magical Moments

"Maa-maaa!" My two-year-old daughter, Alex, called from her crib. I bounded up the stairs, excited to have the whole day to play with her. I was now, officially, a stay-at-home mom. Lucky enough to have the option, I'd made a tough decision and quit my job as a registered nurse.

"Ready for some fun?" I picked up Alex and gave her a tight squeeze, grateful to finally have the time to conquer all the "mommy-and-me" projects I'd collected from parenting magazines. I could never get to them on weekends, and I was ready to catch up. Alex and I would make animal masks out of paper plates in the morning and homemade Play-Doh in the afternoon. For lunch, I'd use cookie cutters to make edible figurines out of American cheese slices. After her nap, we'd make gift wrap using Alex's handprints. My life could finally be full of the magical moments I imagined filled up the days of stay-at-home mothers everywhere.

While singing nursery rhymes, I poured pancake batter into heart-shaped molds, a breakfast that literally showed my love. As I handed Alex her plate, I took a deep breath of satisfaction; she looked so sweet in her new dress and matching hair bow. The day was ours to enjoy. I turned my back for only a second and was shocked to turn back around to find Alex covered in syrup. I'd imagined pushing my princess through the grocery store in her new outfit, while white-haired ladies nodded approvingly over their shopping carts. The fantasy would have to wait. By the time I changed her clothes, cleaned up the breakfast mess, started the laundry, changed a stinky pull-up, and answered two phone calls, I was already way behind schedule. When would I have time to fit in my list of magical moments? On my way out the door, I noticed a note from my husband telling me to please Express Mail the important papers he'd left on his desk to our accountant. The note went on to say that he needed his shirts from the dry cleaners for tomorrow's business trip, and since I no longer worked and had the whole day, could I make his favorite pot roast for dinner?

I sighed. "Well, Alex. We better get moving."

The line at the post office was out the door with only one clerk on duty. Intrigued by all the packaging materials, Alex kept getting away from me to touch everything. I didn't see the harm until . . . *crash*! She knocked over a display of assorted envelopes. I sheepishly cleaned up the mess, thankful a nice man took pity on me and saved my place in line.

From there, we finally headed off to the dry cleaners, but Alex fell asleep in the car. I wanted to run in and leave her napping, but I sensed child abductors lurking everywhere and decided to just go home and let her sleep in peace.

As soon as I turned off the car engine, Alex's eyes shot open and she wailed out a tired cry. As I carried her into the house, I sobbed with her, my high expectations spilling out with my tears. What happened to our perfect day?

When did stay-at-home moms fit in all those quality child-parent activities? I wouldn't even let myself think about my other goals to commit to a regular exercise schedule and start an at-home business. I had really been clueless about this stay-at-home-mom stuff.

Hugging my precious daughter, we rocked and sniffled together. "You're my honey-bear," I whispered, feeling the weight of her sink into me. Her eyes gently shut, and I held her until she fell back asleep in my arms. I stroked the soft hair that curled above her neck and breathed in her smell, a mixture of sweat and maple syrup. Taking a deep breath, I relaxed for the first time that day. I was there with my daughter, forgetting about my to-do list, and it felt good.

Still, it took years for me to realize that such moments were the best and far surpassed the ones I tried to invent with heart-shaped pancakes or processed cheese sculptures. The less I tried to create life's magical moments, the more I was able to notice them when they naturally happened. And they were even more delicious as surprises.

Sherrie Page Najarian

২৯

LIFE LESSON #3:

There are so many amazing and wonderful things that go unnoticed in our lives; it's the small things that we sometimes take for granted without giving a second thought to appreciate their presence. Essential Ingredient #4 touched upon connecting with our authentic self, how motherhood may have redefined us, and the search to nourish our souls. And upon reflection, our choices may also illuminate some of the smaller things in life that, as busy moms, we are often too distracted to notice. When we are in tune, there are numerous events that we may be thankful for that might otherwise go unnoticed. For example, as simplistic as it may sound, if our children ask us to play with them, we can experience their captivation in the moment. As we participate in a meaningful conversation with our spouse or a friend, we truly feel connected and in sync with one another. When we wake up feeling healthy and alert in the morning, we are ready to tackle whatever the day may send our way. Allowing ourselves to truly see the small daily joys in life requires a strong inner voice that says, "Just stop and slow down—enjoy what's around me."

The most sparkling and joyous moments in life are often triggered by the smallest actions or experiences. And to enhance these opportunities, it is important to stay open with a positive frame of mind and outlook on life. This is a conscious decision. It is easy to become overwhelmed by the pressures of our busy lives and then become stuck or drawn into negativity. Complaining, bearing grudges, jealousy, and resentment are all powerful emotions that can drain our energy. And many negative emotions are often contagious.

A busy mom's "in-basket" is never empty, so it is imperative to ask ourselves, what are the important things in our lives? We often recognize the importance of good health and well-being for ourselves and those we love. What about the small things in life? Those of us who live in colder climates can surely appreciate the very first warm day of spring after the long, cold, damp winter months. What about the scent of freshly cut grass or the earthy aroma after a long heavy rain? And ask a coffee drinker about that first sip in the morning, or remember how it feels to smell freshly baked bread—not to mention the first bite after the butter has begun to melt. Collapsing into our bed at night between newly laundered sheets and enjoying the warm comfort of our spouse in bed, we can feel happy that the day went smoothly without any calamities.

These are just a handful of simple pleasures that we may sometimes forget to appreciate. They may not be the most important things in life, but engaging in greater appreciation for the simple areas in life can create a frame of mind that focuses on the aspects that do matter the most.

When greeted by a smiling face and a cheerful voice, whether a child or adult, we typically smile back. We cannot help ourselves—it's a reaction. Expressing our appreciation to others or writing in a journal is one way for us to stay in touch with some of these small things in life that might otherwise pass us by. Taking the time to say "Thank you"—very powerful words if we take the time to use them—not only communicates our appreciation, but can nurture another's self-worth. And if we put on a smile and extend a kindness, these actions will be reflected back to us—most of the time. It may help to remember that everyone's situation is unique. And that person who cut us off on the freeway might just have received some sad or disturbing news about someone they love. Instead of cursing them, we can pattern the reaction of acknowledging they are in a hurry and hope that they will arrive safely at their destination despite their erratic driving! This is an act of kindness that may affect us internally and, ultimately, how we express ourselves to the world.

Voicing our gratitude to others or writing in a journal every day can help us focus on some of the things that we are grateful for in our lives. It can also help us stay centered and may alleviate negativity. Gratitude is mostly about attitude; appreciating the good things that we do have in our lives, instead of dwelling upon those we don't possess, can help us stay focused on what really matters.

Ideas to Appreciate the Small Things in Life

- Don't sweat the small stuff. Sometimes the phrase, "Oh, well" is an easy way to acknowledge a bump in the road, yet allows us to move on quickly to what really matters in life.
- Every night think of a handful of things that happened during the day for which you are grateful.
- Express your appreciation to others.
- Surround yourself with friends who have similar positive traits.
- You may want to keep a daily/weekly "gratitude journal"; when feeling down, consider rereading your thoughts to remind yourself of the important things in life.
- Each time you see a quote, cartoon, or something that represents where you are at in life, paste it in your journal with a comment and the date.

LIFE LESSON #4

Appreciate the Here and Now—Be Present

I'm celebrating my job right now, my life.

Mary J. Blige

✿ Busy Bees

My grandchildren were visiting for the week. They came with a written calendar of events. Pick-up times and drop-off times. I was in charge of keeping them busy and on schedule. I'm not good at either. As an older adult, I manage to keep occupied, but I don't think I'm busy. My dog doesn't care if he's busy. He just wants his walk twice a day. And my cats, in between long naps, avoid being busy. I do not have a busy house, though I have a business in my home. I wasn't certain how my grandchildren would react to the lack of activity, to the abundance of free time. "What are we doing today?" they would ask. "I don't know," I'd answer.

I could see by their faces it was not the expected reply. Somehow we managed to pass the day. We did some staring at the squirrels running up the tree. We took the dog for a walk and played ball with him. We sat on rocking chairs watching people walk up and down the street, and we wondered aloud where they were going. We spent some time talking to the parakeet in his cage and took some long walks around the corner and up the block. We drew some chalk pictures on the sidewalk, and for an hour or two, we just sat being bored. But that was okay, because in the free-time zone, you don't have to be entertaining or exciting or wonderful all the time. Or busy. You can just be.

But kids today are accustomed to being like busy bees. They're busy from the time they get up until the time they go to bed. And it's a long day. Some of them get up at 7:00 AM and do not go to bed until 10:00 or 11:00 PM. Not only are they busy at school, but they are busy with after-school activities, and with keeping up with their friends who are also busy. They do a lot of traveling in cars, keeping busy going from one house to another to fulfill play-dates. Play is no longer spontaneous. It's scheduled, as are dance classes, soccer and baseball, religious classes, and add to the itinerary, doctor's and dentist's appointments.

There is little free time. Unscheduled time is a rare treasure, on the brink of becoming extinct. People fear it, run from it, and avoid it. One morning during my weekend in charge of the children, we lay in my king-size bed all morning deciding what to do with the day. We thought about it a long time. We watched television. We talked. We told each other things we didn't have time to share before. We explored our feelings about the day and about some problems disturbing us. We even dared to be silent with each other. Nobody moved to get dressed. Nobody made a telephone call to a friend. We didn't know what was going on outside the house. We didn't even care. We were in the free-time zone, the no-time zone, the no-clock, no-schedule, no-pressure zone, where it didn't matter if there's nothing to do. And no place to go.

The free-time zone—where imagination, creativity and truth roam unconfined, at last.

Harriet May Savitz

❧

"Retrospect"

Today I left the small fingerprints on the windowpane. I left the toy in the corner and the dishes undone. I rocked her extra long as she lay peacefully on my breast.

Today I held her hand as we walked the soon-to-be familiar path to her first day at school. She smiled and waved good-bye. She didn't see the tear in my eye or feel the lump in my throat. Later, I showed her the way home and listened to every little thing that excited her heart.

Today she met her first young love. He held her hand in his while his eyes spoke a thousand words of love. His future intertwined with hers as their hearts beat as one. I shared her joy. She couldn't see the tear in my eye or feel the lump in my throat.

Today was her day. A cap, a gown, a tassel! A celebration

of all she had become and all she had to offer. A day of promise, new beginnings, and dreams. *Where had my little girl gone?* I wanted to hold her against my breast and rock her extra long.

Today was their day. The white gown, the music, the roses, the lilies, and the love. I let go of her hand. Yet my arms remained open. This day of joy! She didn't see the tear in my eye or feel the lump in my throat.

Today was our day. God's gift to them. Their gift to each other. Their gift to us. So small, so sleepy, so perfect, so beautiful. I took her in my arms. Her little fingers curled around mine. I was older now—a grandmother! I held her against my breast and rocked her extra long.

Today was my day. She held me against her breast and rocked me extra long. I had left fingerprints in her life. She listened as I told her of my pain. Today she was there to help me home. Today I couldn't see the tear in her eye or feel the lump in her throat.

Today she placed a rose in my hand. She remembered the fragrance of life and the bond we shared. Today she placed a white lily on my grave while she held a small hand in hers.

Today she held her against her breast and rocked her extra long. God saw the tears in their eyes and felt the lumps in their throats. He wrapped his loving arms around them and rocked them extra long.

Glorianne M. Swenson

LIFE LESSON #4:

The concept of "staying present" is easier said than done. We are swept away on a regular basis by what's happening next—always rushing, looking at the time, trying to prepare for what is to come.

For stay-at-home moms with young children, the days can seem rather stagnant, filled with feedings and diaper changes—or with school-age children, filled with dance classes, and carpool trips. When experiencing this, it's difficult to move on from the mind-set, "When they get older, it will get easier," therefore making it challenging to stay present and appreciate the here and now. We may enjoy moments when we take in the precious times of rocking our babies to sleep—in awe of our little ones' beautiful faces, and their magnificent tiny fingers. But in order to create more experiences such as this, we may need to make a conscious decision to stay more present and appreciate life moment to moment.

When our kids are school-age or teenagers, we are typically rushing around to the point where our heads feel like they're spinning. Aside from school, there are the extracurricular activities, sporting events, and the daily errands that need addressing. While we are in the thick of these busy days, taking mental pictures of our daughter running down the soccer field or our son standing at the plate anxious to hit the ball, there are fleeting moments to appreciate. Stay present, because as we know, these amazing times fly by so incredibly fast. And remember, we can always keep these loving images by pulling out albums and memory scrapbooks to remind us again of those times.

Some of us integrate the ability to appreciate the here and now quite well within our busy days. For those of us who are still in the process of honing this skill, we may need to make cognizant efforts to appreciate today. Another way to accomplish staying in the present is to create a greater connection with our physical being. The powerful effect of purposeful breathing, connecting with nature, or appreciating the small things in life are all avenues that may help us stay present more frequently throughout our days. Experiencing physical activities, for example, exercising, stretching, and receiving or giving a massage are additional ways to stay in the moment.

The years seem to quickly pass by in this age of high technology and fast-paced living, and before we know it, our kids are off on their own. It is the moments when we are truly present that seem to stay with us the longest—almost as if we have "snapshot pictures" that are forever entrenched in our hearts and minds. These are the experiences that can stay with us forever.

When revisiting the Life Lessons throughout this book, we can see they are all windows that can contribute toward us thriving throughout our busy days. When nurturing ourselves, we are better equipped to nurture our families. When figuring out and implementing our parenting philosophy, it can make the days run more smoothly and contribute toward our children achieving a healthier and more balanced life. Implementing creative solutions and keeping organized homes can give us sanity. When we feed our souls and solicit help, this can help us live each day to the fullest. Then ultimately, when we make time to slow down, it can afford us the opportunity to cherish the meaningful moments in our lives as we continue on with our incredible journey of life as busy moms.

We feel that the most important tips to take away from the Life Lessons presented to our readers—busy moms—are to:

- Finish reviewing the book.
- Put the book down.
- And do something for you!

Also, remember: Organizing your life creates a better quality of life for you and your family!

1. Before putting this book down, notice what you hear, smell, feel, and see, and take one minute to be present.
2. Take a couple of minutes to recall the last warm, loving touch you received and appreciate that moment.

Notes

ESSENTIAL INGREDIENT #1: Life Lesson #1

1. U.S. Census Bureau, "Two Married Parents the Norm" (June 12, 2004). *http://www.census.gov/population/www//socdemo/hh-fam.*
2. Robo, Regina M. "Dream Job: Stay-at-Home Mom." *Salary.com. http://www.salary.com/careers/layouthtmls/crel_display_Cat10_Ser253_Par358.html.*
3. Ibid.

ESSENTIAL INGREDIENT #4: Life Lesson #2

1. Taylor, S. E., Klein, L. C., Lewis, B. P., Gruenewald, T. L., Gurung, R. A. R., & Updegraff, J. A. (2000). "Female Responses to Stress: Tend and Befriend, Not Fight or Flight." *Psychological Review* 107 (3): 411–429.

ESSENTIAL INGREDIENT #4: Life Lesson #3

1. Estroff Marano, Hara. (2003). "The Goals that Guide Us." *Psyched for Success* (doc. 2890).

ESSENTIAL INGREDIENT #4: Life Lesson #4

1. Source for quotation at the beginning of this chapter: Kübler-Ross, Elisabeth. *www.elisabethkublerross.com* and *www.ekrfoundation.org.*

ESSENTIAL INGREDIENT #5: Life Lesson #1

1. Swenson, Richard A. "Margin: Restoring Emotional, Physical, Financial, and Time Reserves to Overloaded Lives." *NavPress* (June 1992).
2. Winston, Stephanie. "Best Organizing Tips: Quick, Simple Ways to

Get Organized and Get on with Your Life." *Fireside* (January 11, 2006), p. 30.

ESSENTIAL INGREDIENT #5: Life Lesson #2

1. Baron, Kelly. "Hurry Up and Wait." *Forbes*, October 16, 2000. Volume 166, issue 1, p. 158.

ESSENTIAL INGREDIENT #6: Life Lesson #1

1. The American College of Obstetricians and Gynecologists (ACOG). "Spotlight on Postpartum Depression." ACOG Co-Sponsors National Depression Screening Day, 2005 Marks First-Time Focus on Postpartum Depression (September 30, 2005). *http://www.acog.org/from_home/publications/press_releases/nr09-30-05-2.cfm*
2. Ibid.

ESSENTIAL INGREDIENT #7: Life Lesson #1

1. *holistic-online.com. "Importance of Breathing." http://www.holistic-online.com/Yoga/hol_yoga_breathing_Importance.htm.*
2. Ibid.
3. Evans, Diane. "Breathing exercises can relieve stress." Knight Ridder/Tribune Service, April 25, 2003.
4. Ibid.
5. Ibid.

ESSENTIAL INGREDIENT #7: Life Lesson #2

1. Robbins, Irma. "Native American healing practices and counseling." *Journal of Humanistic Counseling, Education and Development*, March 22, 2004.
2. Fosdick, Dean. "Designer Touts Healing Power of Gardening." Associated Press (AP) Online, April 2, 2003.

More Chicken Soup?

Many of the stories and poems you have read in this book were submitted by readers like you who had read earlier *Chicken Soup for the Soul* books. We publish many *Chicken Soup for the Soul* books every year. We invite you to contribute a story to one of these future volumes.

Stories may be up to 1,200 words and must uplift or inspire. You may submit an original piece, something you have read, or your favorite quotation on your refrigerator door.

To obtain a copy of our submission guidelines and a listing of upcoming *Chicken Soup* books, please write, fax, or check our website.

Please send your submissions to:

website: *www.chickensoup.com*
Chicken Soup for the Soul
P.O. Box 30880
Santa Barbara, CA 93130
fax: 805-563-2945

Just send a copy of your stories and other pieces to the above address.

We will be sure that both you and the author are credited for your submission.

For information about speaking engagements, other books, audiotapes, workshops, and training programs, please contact any of our authors directly.

Supporting Others

In the spirit of supporting others, a portion of the proceeds from *Life Lessons for Busy Moms* will be donated to the **EB Medical Research Foundation**.

The **EB Medical Research Foundation** was established in 1991 to fund the Stanford University School of Medicine in their continued research and study of a rare genetic disorder called epidermolysis bullosa (EB).

There are several forms of this inherited blistering skin disease, ranging from mild to the severely disabling and life threatening. It affects all ethnicities—as many as 500,000 people worldwide. Until recently, children born with one of the two lethal forms of the disease had no expectation of a normal life.

The **EB Medical Research Foundation** is uniquely run on a volunteer basis; it donates 99 percent of its contributions directly to this program. In the last few years Stanford's scientists have made great strides with their gene therapy research. And as a result, gene correction for one of the two lethal forms of this disease is now possible.

It is our privilege to donate a portion of the proceeds from *Life Lessons for Busy Moms* to the **EB Medical Research**

Foundation for their support of Stanford University School of Medicine as they continue to study and research this tragic disease.

If you would like more information please contact:

Andrea Pett-Joseph
Mailing & Administrative Offices
EB Medical Research Foundation
8909 W. Olympic Blvd. # 222
Beverly Hills, CA 90211
Phone: 310-979-8078
E-mail: a.pett@bgent.com
www.ebkids.org

Who Is Jack Canfield?

Jack Canfield is the cocreator and editor of the Chicken Soup for the Soul series, which *Time* magazine has called "the publishing phenomenon of the decade." The series now has 105 titles with over 100 million copies in print in forty-one languages. Jack is also the coauthor of eight other bestselling books including *The Success Principles: How to Get from Where You Are to Where You Want to Be*, *Dare to Win*, *The Aladdin Factor*, *You've Got to Read This Book*, and *The Power of Focus: How to Hit Your Business and Personal and Financial Targets with Absolute Certainty*.

Jack has recently developed a telephone coaching program and an online coaching program based on his most recent book *The Success Principles*. He also offers a seven-day Breakthrough to Success seminar every summer, which attracts 400 people from fifteen countries around the world.

Jack has conducted intensive personal and professional development seminars on the principles of success for over 900,000 people in twenty-one countries around the world. He has spoken to hundreds of thousands of others at numerous conferences and conventions and has been seen by millions of viewers on national television shows such as *The Today Show*, *Fox and Friends*, *Inside Edition*, *Hard Copy*, CNN's *Talk Back Live*, *20/20*, *Eye to Eye*, the *NBC Nightly News*, and the *CBS Evening News*.

Jack is the recipient of many awards and honors, including three honorary doctorates and a Guinness World Records Certificate for having seven books from the Chicken Soup for the Soul series appearing on the *New York Times* bestseller list on May 24, 1998.

To write to Jack or for inquiries about Jack as a speaker, his coaching programs, or his seminars, use the following contact information:

The Canfield Companies
P.O. Box 30880 • Santa Barbara, CA 93130
phone: 805-563-2935 • fax: 805-563-2945
E-mail: info@jackcanfield.com or
visit his website at www.jackcanfield.com

Who Is Mark Victor Hansen?

In the area of human potential, no one is more respected than Mark Victor Hansen. For more than thirty years, Mark has focused solely on helping people from all walks of life reshape their personal vision of what's possible. His powerful messages of possibility, opportunity, and action have created powerful change in thousands of organizations and millions of individuals worldwide.

He is a sought-after keynote speaker, bestselling author, and marketing maven. Mark's credentials include a lifetime of entrepreneurial success and an extensive academic background. He is a prolific writer with many bestselling books, such as *The One Minute Millionaire*, *Cracking the Millionaire Code*, *How to Make the Rest of Your Life the Best of Your Life*, *The Power of Focus*, *The Aladdin Factor*, and *Dare to Win*, in addition to the Chicken Soup for the Soul series. Mark has made a profound influence through his library of audios, videos, and articles in the areas of big thinking, sales achievement, wealth building, publishing success, and personal and professional development.

Mark is the founder of the MEGA Seminar Series. MEGA Book Marketing University and Building Your MEGA Speaking Empire are annual conferences where Mark coaches and teaches new and aspiring authors, speakers, and experts on building lucrative publishing and speaking careers. Other MEGA events include MEGA Info-Marketing and My MEGA Life.

As a philanthropist and humanitarian, Mark works tirelessly for organizations such as Habitat for Humanity, American Red Cross, March of Dimes, Childhelp USA, and many others. He is the recipient of numerous awards that honor his entrepreneurial spirit, philanthropic heart, and business acumen. He is a lifetime member of the Horatio Alger Association of Distinguished Americans, an organization that honored Mark with the prestigious Horatio Alger Award for his extraordinary life achievements.

Mark Victor Hansen is an enthusiastic crusader of what's possible and is driven to make the world a better place.

Mark Victor Hansen & Associates, Inc.

P.O. Box 7665 • Newport Beach, CA 92658

phone: 949-764-2640 • fax: 949-722-6912

www.markvictorhansen.com

Who Is Lynn Benson?

Lynn Benson, "mommy expert" and president of Delphi Health Products, Inc., has coauthored BioBinder™ *Cherished Memories: The Story of My Life* and *The Senior Organizer.* Prior to her position at Delphi, Lynn's career began in the child care field. Starting off as a preschool teacher, she was then promoted to center director, which enabled her to work closely with busy moms and support them within all aspects of their challenging days and life issues. Lynn eventually became a regional director, overseeing the operations of the national multiunit intergenerational company that cared for children and elders. During this time, she spent countless hours creating and organizing systems to ensure the quality of the intergenerational curriculum and daily procedures.

Lynn also holds a master's degree in social work and carries a diverse and significant background working with children, families, and seniors. While working with these families in a therapeutic environment, she was also a strong advocate to help further their quality of life. And, in an effort to improve communications within families and communities, Lynn gave numerous seminars on the topic of "conflict resolution."

Lynn is a member of the National Association of Professional Organizers (NAPO) and lives and breathes the lifestyle of a busy mom—she is the mother of two young children.

For more information on Lynn and her organizing books and products, please visit:

www.biobinders.com
Phone: 800-791-8071
Fax: 818-784-9437

Who Is Debby Bitticks?

Debby Bitticks, a nationally recognized intergenerational expert, and CEO of Delphi Health Products, Inc., has coauthored BioBinder™ *Cherished Memories: The Story of My Life, The Senior Organizer* and *Time Efficiency Makeover.*

Prior to her position at Delphi, Debby was the founder and CEO of a national multiunit intergenerational company. Her innovative curriculums and programs were designed to educate, nurture, and provide day care for both children and elders. Debby was a pioneer in recognizing the multitude of benefits when children and elders interacted with one another. As an educational therapist Debby also designed special programs for children with visual perceptual disorders and dyslexia.

Debby provided busy parents with a "Family Resource Center" to assist them with parenting issues, family issues, and balancing life's competing priorities. During this time, Debby was raising her own four daughters and implementing her organizing concepts, educational philosophies, and strategies.

A recognized expert, Debby has presented and spoken at the National Council on Aging (NCOA) in Washington, DC, on intergenerational care, and has appeared on CBS, NBC, ABC, Fox, CNN Financial News, and other cable shows, as well as giving numerous national radio interviews. Debby has also appeared on QVC with BioBinder™ *Cherished Memories: The Story of My Life.*

She has received the prestigious Blue Chip Enterprise Award given by the U.S. Chamber of Commerce and Connecticut Mutual Life Insurance Company. Debby is a member of the National Association of Professional Organizers (NAPO) and National Council on the Aging (NCOA).

Debby sits on the board of Vital Options International, a nonprofit organization, and TeleSupport Cancer Network. She also actively supports many other worthwhile charities, personally and through donations from purchases of her company's products.

For more information on Debby and her full line of organizing books and products, please visit:

www.biobinders.com
Phone: 800-791-8071
Fax: 818-784-9437

Who Is Dorothy Breininger?

Dorothy Breininger, America's most trusted professional organizer and CEO of the Center for Organization, devotes her life to teaching people how to design a life they love—through organizing pace (time), face (energy and enthusiasm for life), space (office or environment), and grace (gratitude and spirit).

Dorothy served on the board of directors for the National Association of Professional Organizers (NAPO) and is a member of the National Study Group on Chronic Disorganization (NSGCD). National speaking favorite and product spokesperson, Dorothy has appeared as an expert on the *Today Show* and the *Dr. Phil Show*, and has been featured in *Forbes*, *Woman's Day*, *Fast Company*, and *Entrepreneur* magazines.

Among other books, Dorothy is coauthor of *Time Efficiency Makeover*—a workbook for procrastinators—and *The Senior Organizer*. Dorothy's compassionate and successful work with everyone from busy moms to seniors, coupled with her willingness to give her time to worthwhile events and charities, has earned her a commendation by the Los Angeles County Board of Supervisors and the National Small Business Champion of the Year Award from the Small Business Association.

The Center for Organization services include:
- Home and office organization
- Corporate organization
- Hoarding and packrat overhauls
- Group coaching calls
- Individual coaching calls
- Private coaching
- Keynotes, seminars, and workshops
- Separation coaching
- Personal assisting
- Private goal setting sessions

Classes and coaching on how to become a professional organizer

For more information on Dorothy, please visit:
www.centerfororganization.com
Phone: 800-660-GOAL
Fax: 818-597-0618

Contributors

Aaron Bacall has graduate degrees in organic chemistry as well as in educational administration and supervision from New York University. He has been a pharmaceutical research chemist, teacher, and cartoonist. He has sold his cartoons to most national publications and has had seven books of his cartoons published. Currently he is a college coordinator for continuing education. He continues to create and sell his cartoons and is writing a script for a stage play as well.

Sherry Bishop is originally from Atlanta, Georgia, but now lives and writes in New York City. She is a graduate of the University of Georgia and also holds an MA in theater from Florida State University. In addition to a variety of articles, Sherry has also written a number of plays. E-mail her at sbishop@nvbb.net.

Heather Black is a writer who lives in Gainesville, Florida.

Chrissy Boylan is a busy at-home mom to her two young daughters and a writer in her spare time. She lives with her husband and children in northern Virginia, where her previous work has appeared in the *Washington Post*.

Kimberly Edwina Campbell's work has been accepted by *Pockets, Kid Zone, On the Line, Cadet Quest, Shine Brightly, Writer's Digest, The Institute of Chicken's Literature*, and Blooming Tree Press (SUMMER SHORTS, June 2006). Her first nonfiction book is a biography of Newbery author Richard Peck (Enslow, Fall 2007). She has won a handful of national and regional writing competitions. Visit her website at www.KimberlyCampbell.net.

As a seasoned professional organizer in Arlington, Virginia, **C. Lee Cawley** loves to transform peoples' lives with simple solutions. In addition to running her company, Simplify You, Inc., C. Lee keeps busy with her many volunteer activities and reading and relaxing with her husband, Tom, and daughter, Lydia. Contact her at info@simplifyou.com.

Lorilee Craker speaks for Mothers of Preschoolers (MOPS) groups and at other events for mothers. She is the author of four books, including *Just Give Me a Little Piece of Quiet* and *We Should Do This More Often*. She lives in Grand Rapids, Michigan, with her husband and three children.

Lauren Martin Culp is the married mother of two, an educator, author, and licensed marriage and family therapist in private practice in Santa Monica, California, where she integrates the latest research in neurobiology into her work. Please e-mail her at Lauren@Laurenculp.com.

Mimi Greenwood Knight is a freelance writer and artist in residence in the public school system. She lives in southern Louisiana with her husband and four children, enjoys gardening, Bible study, and the lost art of letter writing. Mimi is currently compiling a collection of essays about her adventures in motherhood. Give her a ring at djknight@airmail.net.

Jonny Hawkins has had thousands of cartoons published in hundreds of places over the last twenty years. He has his own calendars—"Medical Cartoon-A-Day," "Fishing Cartoon-A-Day," and "Cartoons for Teachers." His books, *A Tackle Box of Fishing Funnies, The Awesome Book of Heavenly Humor,* and *Laughter from the Pearly Gates* are in stores also. He can be reached at jonnyhawkins2nz@yahoo.com.

Angela Jones received her BA from the University of Minnesota Duluth in 1998 and her MA from Central Michigan University in 2000. Currently she is a stay-at-home mom and has learned several life lessons from her two busy preschoolers, Dominic and Dana. Angela resides in northern Minnesota with her husband, Darin.

Terri L. Knight received her BA in psychology from Bowling Green State University (BGSU) and her paralegal certificate from Lakeland Community College. She writes fiction and nonfiction and is working on an essay, several short stories, and her first novel, *Nicole*. Her hobbies include cooking, jogging, and reading. She can be reached at r280ac@msn.com.

Karen Krugman is a professional organizer living and working in New York City with her two daughters. She specializes in organizing families and home offices. She is currently working on a guide to organizing paperwork for the home. She can be reached at cluttersos@aol.com.

Veneta Leonard is a very happy stay-at-home mother. She has been married for more than eleven years and has eight beautiful children. She currently resides in Illinois and is very involved in her faith and her family.

Pam McCutcheon is married and has two boys. She owns "The Clutter Cutter" professional organizing service in Wichita, Kansas. She specializes in chronic disorganization and organizing estates. Pam enjoys working puzzles, going to garage sales, and working in ministry. You may e-mail her at mccutcheon_pam@thecluttercutter.com.

Cheryl Mills lives in Cumming, Georgia, with her husband and four children. She enjoys good books, good movies, and vacations with her family. She fills the little bit of spare time she has with writing essays, articles, short stories, and novels. Please e-mail her at mills.cheryl@gmail.com.

Sherrie Page Najarian is a registered nurse and freelance writer who lives in Richmond, Virginia. She enjoys skiing, long walks, and hanging out with her family. Her favorite pastime is finding cool things to do around the city of Richmond. She is currently writing a young adult novel.

Catherine Newman wrote the award-winning memoir, *Waiting for Birdy*. She also authors *Dalai Mama*, a weekly column at *wondertime.com*, and *Bringing Up Ben and Birdy* at *babycenter.com*, in which parts of this essay were originally published. She lives with her family in Amherst, Massachusetts. Please go to www.benandbirdy.blogspot.com.

Phyllis Nutkis taught preschool and kindergarten for fifteen years before finally "graduating" in 2004. She currently works as a grant writer for a social service agency and also writes for various publications, including *Chicago Parent* magazine. She and her husband have three children and two grandchildren. E-mail her at Phyllis.Nutkis@gmail.com.

Natalie Orta is the proud mother of Daniel and Teresa, who have made it into their teenage years relatively unscathed. She enjoys gardening, swimming, hiking, traveling, and the simple pleasures of life.

Stephanie Piro lives in New Hampshire with her husband, daughter, and three cats. She is one of King Features' team of women cartoonists, "Six Chix" (she is the Saturday chick!). Her single-panel, *Fair Game*, appears in newspapers and on her website at www.stephaniepiro.com. She also designs gift items for her company Strip T's. Contact her at piro@worldpath.net or by mail at P.O. Box 605, Farmington, NH 03835.

Dan Reynolds's cartoon, *Reynolds Unwrapped*, is seen every day on Universal Press Syndicate's site http://www.ucomics.com/reynoldsunwrapped/index.phtml. He has four nationally published cartoon books with Andrews McMeel

Publishing. His work is seen across the United States on greeting cards and in every issue of *Reader's Digest*. Dan's work has appeared on *The Sopranos*. Please reach Dan at cartoonist89@hotmail.com.

Forbes Riley is a world-renowned TV host, actress, and public speaker. Originally from New York, she currently resides with her twins and husband in Los Angeles. Forbes is working on publishing her first book.

Cartoonist **Dan Rosandich** operates his extensive online catalog of cartoons, which can be licensed for any specific usage, with fees based upon various factors. Visit www.danscartoons.com.

Harriet May Savitz is an award-winning author of reissued groundbreaking books about the disabled (for readers twelve years and up). Among them are *Run, Don't Walk* (which was produced by Henry Winkler as an ABC Afterschool Special), *The Bullies and Me, A Girl's Best Friend*, and *Swimmer* (fiction, for readers eight to twelve). You can contact her at www.harrietmaysavitz.com or hmaysavitz@aol.com.

Heidi N. Schulz is an organizing consultant from Santa Barbara, California. Balancing her work with chronically disorganized individuals, Heidi skis "off piste" in search of powder snow, studies a wolf pack in Canada, and kayaks in the Baja. One day, Heidi hopes to capture some of these adventures on paper. Please e-mail her at organize-heidischulz@cox.net.

Esther Simon, professional organizer, National Association of Professional Organizers (NAPO) member, and mother of seven, helps her clients deal with time management, clutter, space planning, kosher kitchens, and file systems in homes and offices. She has given workshops and lectures on time management and organizational skills throughout the greater Los Angeles area. Contact Esther at tradhomorg@aol.com.

Joyce Stark lives in northeast Scotland and splits her time between writing and working for the Community Mental Health Team. She is currently writing a children's serial to promote early learning of a second language and a cookbook entitled *You Put WHAT in It?*

Jean Stewart, writer and editor in Mission Viejo, California, has been married for forty-five years, is the mother of twin daughters and a grandmother of two. Her most recent articles are in *ByLine* magazine and the *Orange County Register*. Jean's stories are included in *Chicken Soup for Father & Daughter, Horse Lovers II*, and *Cup of Comfort for Women in Love*.

Glorianne M. Swenson is a Minnesota-based freelance writer and small business owner of Gloribks. Her genre includes creative nonfiction memoirs, devotionals, poetry, and children's picture book manuscripts. She is a wife, mother, and grandmother, and enjoys singing, piano, geneaology, and antiquing. She may be e-mailed at gloribks@charter.net.

Sabrina A. Taylor lives in Medford, Oregon, with her two wonderful daughters, Mikayla and Shyla, and her husband, Todd. Formerly a CAN, she now stays home to care for her children. You can reach her at mommy_bri@hotmail.com.

Being a mother is one of **Stephanie Welcher Thompson**'s greatest blessings. She's a stay-at-home mom who writes when she's apart from daughter, Micah, and husband, Michael. Read her in *Guideposts, Angels on Earth, Positive Thinking, Sweet 16,* and *Chicken Soup and Soul Matters.* Reach her at P.O. Box 1502, Edmond, OK 73083 or stephanie@stateofchange.net.

Tiffany Todd-Fitch was dragged to small-town Mississippi from Dallas in 2001. When not chasing her four wild munchkins through the house, she writes about the state she has come to love. Her essays can be heard on *Mississippi Public Broadcasting* or read in the *Jackson Free Press.* She can be reached by e-mail at tiffitch@bellsouth.net.

Kate Varness, stay-at-home mom of three, understands the challenges of keeping up with preschoolers' messes. She is a member of the National Association of Professional Organizers (NAPO) and a speaker for moms' groups. Kate enjoys scrapbooking and reading, and has a keen interest in personality type theory. E-mail her at kkvarness@hotmail.com.

Barbara Whipple received her BA from Dartmouth College in 1985. She is a professional organizer and mother of two young sons, Connor and Kyle. Barbara enjoys traveling, skiing, reading, and writing. She plans to write her own book one day. Please e-mail her at bwhipple@comcast.net.

Gillian White is a California implant who thanks her husband for his dedicated love and commitment, which is the bedrock of their life together. His devotion, coupled with the support of family both near and far, has encouraged her to pursue the dreams and creative endeavors of her heart.

Ferida Wolff is the author of *The Adventures of Swamp Woman: Menopause Essays on the Edge* and sixteen books for children. She teaches meditation and stretching and speaks at schools. Her garden inspires many of her essays. Please visit her website at www.feridawolff.com or contact her at feridawolff@msn.com.

Thousands of **Bob Zahn**'s cartoons have been published in all the leading publications. He has more than a thousand greeting cards to his credit. Several of his humor books have been published. His e-mail address is zahntoons@aol.com.

Permissions *(continued from page iv)*

How Did Mama Do It? Reprinted by permission of Meredith Knight. ©2002 Meredith Knight.

Blended and Balanced. Reprinted by permission of Gillian Drake-White. ©2006 Gillian Drake-White.

A Hug a Day. Reprinted by permission of Veneta Leonard. ©2006 Veneta Leonard.

A Gift of Running. Reprinted by permission of Sherry Bishop. ©1999 Sherry Bishop.

Juggling Act. Reprinted by permission of Phyllis L. Nutkis. ©2006 Phyllis L. Nutkis.

When Life Gives You Lemons. Reprinted by permission of Meredith Knight. ©1999 Meredith Knight.

Picking Your Battles. Excerpted from *Wide-Eyed Wonder Years.* Lorilee Craker and Fleming H. Revell, a division of Baker Publishing Group. ©2006.

Three Red Xs. Reprinted by permission of Tiffany Todd-Fitch. ©2006 Tiffany Todd-Fitch.

A Lesson in Compromise. Reprinted by permission of Catherine Newman. ©2006 Catherine Newman.

Why Puppies and Babies Go So Well Together. Reprinted by permission of Forbes Riley. ©2006 Forbes Riley.

Early-Morning Rush. Reprinted by permission of Esther Simon. ©2006 Esther Simon.

The Treasure Bag. Reprinted by permission of Karen Lynn Krugman. ©2006 Karen Lynn Krugman.

Ending Toy Room Cleanup Trauma. Reprinted by permission of Kathryn Kitzmann Varness. ©2005 Kathryn Kitzmann Varness.

Missy's Menagerie. Reprinted by permission of Heidi N. Schulz. ©2006 Heidi N. Schulz.

The Art of Connection: My Daughter and Myself. Reprinted by permission of Lauren Martin Culp. ©2006 Lauren Martin Culp.

You know you're a mom when . . . Reprinted by permission of Angela Jean Jones. ©2005 Angela Jean Jones.